The Great American Comedy Scene

William and Rhoda Cahn

MONARCH

Contents

Introduction

There are many ways of looking at comedy.

"The urge to laugh, in civilized man, seems to be almost as irrepressible as the urges of hunger and sex."—A psychiatrist

"When a chimp is playful and happy, it does not smile as we do."—A zookeeper

"Humor is one of the best safety valves."—A comedian

"I mean, what the hell is there to laugh at. . . . People see nothing funny in pollution, overpopulation, and Vietnam."—A nightclub owner

"Our age desperately needs fun and nonsense."—A great newspaper

"When you have people who cannot laugh at people in power—then you're in trouble."—An anthropologist

"Somehow slipping on a banana peel *is* funny."—Another comedian

There are many points of view. For example, mine:

Laughter is a peculiarly human bond of friendship which can help unite the past with the present; and people of all languages, ages, and points of view.

WILLIAM CAHN

I

He Made George Washington Laugh

"Vot iss id has two feet, has fedders all ofer id, und barks like a dog?"

"I give up."

"A chicgen."

"Why, a chicken doesn't bark like a dog!"

"I know id. I chust pud id in to make id hard!"

People laughed at Sam Bernard's comedy of a past generation. But no comedian is ever dead certain what makes an audience laugh.

Laughing is the expression of merriment by convulsive sounds accompanied by opening the mouth and wrinkling the face. People laughed when W. C. Fields solemnly explained away his drinking habits by saying that he didn't believe in "dining on an empty stomach." They laughed when Gracie Allen explained that the reason why she drives with the emergency brake on is in case there is an emergency. They laughed, too, at Henry Morgan's story of how he was born of mixed parents. His mother was a woman and his father was a man.

From among the many comic personalities who appear on TV and in the motion pictures, there are certain ones who have made millions of people want to laugh. Currently, the range of laugh-provoking comics includes diverse personalities and types of comic style. There is the clown who saves a situation by assuming yet another inhuman pose, such as Lucille Ball; the braggart,

9

for example, uses body language, stylized gestures, and absurd schemes—such as Fonzi does—to make odd things occur. A caricature personality, like Archie Bunker or Maude, coming from the familiarity of a home situation, provokes a different kind of laughter. The country clod who speaks slowly and eventually outwits the sophisticated, urban personality, may be like Redd Foxx or Tommy Smothers.

When stand-up comics such as Bob Hope or Jack Benny, Milton Berle, George Burns or Johnny Carson, make one funny observation after another in rapid succession, it sets people laughing from coast to coast. But it was not always this way in America. In the early days of our country, especially in New England, the Puritan culture was opposed to the theater.

When some English actors tried to organize a theater in New England back in 1750, there was a small riot and the Massachusetts General Court sternly reaffirmed its traditional ban on "public stage plays, interludes and other theatrical entertainments." With the Puritanical finger leveled in their direction, the theaters that existed found the going difficult.

Further trouble resulted in 1774 when the Continental Congress ordered the closing of all places of public amusement. There was a revolution to be won. The edict was against "horse racing, and all kinds of gamery, cock fighting, exhibitions of shews, plays, and other expensive Diversions and Entertainments."

A dozen years later, however, the reopened theater was ready for a new style. Second-rate imitations of English theater were no longer suitable. This probably accounts for the reception given to the play, *The Contrast*, by Royall Tyler. The play held up to ridicule "corrupt and frivolous practices of the old world of fashion contrasted with the sturdy, vigorous forthrightness of new America."

It was the first American play produced by an American, written by an American, and played by Americans with an American theme. The main character in the play was Jonathan, a humorous Yankee servant, played by Thomas Wignell.

Although *The Contrast* was given to much talking and little action, it was well received by the theater-going public in the small, slowly growing city of New York. It played five times in quick succession.

Wignell, who came to America from England at the outbreak of

George Washington en-
joyed going to the theater
and was a fan of Thomas
Wignell, the first major
American comedian.

The first native American
comedy was The Contrast.
The copy of The Contrast
was the personal possession
of Washington, whose sig-
nature appears on it.

[Facsimile, slightly reduced]

THE

CONTRAST,

A

COMEDY;

IN FIVE ACTS:

WRITTEN BY A
CITIZEN OF THE UNITED STATES;

Performed with Applaufe at the Theatres in NEW-YORK,
PHILADELPHIA, and MARYLAND;

AND PUBLISHED (under an Affignment of the Copy-Right) BY
THOMAS WIGNELL.

Primus ego in patriam
Aonio——deduxi vertice Mufas.
VIRGIL.
(Imitated.)

Firft on our fhores I try THALIA's powers,
And bid the laughing, ufeful Maid be ours.

PHILADELPHIA:

FROM THE PRESS OF PRICHARD & HALL, IN MARKET STREET,
BETWEEN SECOND AND FRONT STREETS.

M. DCC. XC.

the Revolutionary War, was a man below ordinary height with a
slight stoop of the shoulder. According to one historian of the era,
"Wignell was athletic with handsomely formed lower extremi-
ties, the knees a little curved inward, and feet remarkably small.
His large blue eyes were rich in expression, and his comedy was
luxuriant in humor, but always faithful to his author. He was a
comic actor, not a buffoon."

In the part of a low-comedy servant, Wignell would shuffle
about the stage whittling sticks, exclaiming frequently "Tarna-
tion," or "I vum," and calling himself "the true-born son of liberty." Wignell's character was Jonathan, the shrewd, half-edu-
cated Yankee servant who set a pattern for future Jonathans for
many years to come.

With these and other roles Wignell attracted the attention of

President George Washington, a devoted fan of the theater. Perhaps Tom Wignell's career reached its highest point on the night of November 24, 1789, when a play, *Poor Soldier*, in which he was the main comic character, was presented to the public. There was a great furor when it was learned that a party including President Washington had made reservations for the evening performance. Special preparations were made to receive the beloved hero of the Revolutionary War.

Joseph Jefferson I was one of our first popular comedians and helped continue the Yankee character originated by Tom Wignell. He is pictured (left) in a scene from an early play, A Budget of Blunders.

According to the records of the time, Washington sat very stiff and stern in his box watching the comedy. When the final curtain fell and the President gave not the slightest indication of having been amused, Wignell took the opportunity of a curtain call to present a brief and flowery verse dedicated to the first president.

The poem described Washington as "a man who fought to free the land from woe," etc. As the reading approached its conclusion, Washington remained as stiff and stern as before, perhaps stiffer.

Wignell sensed the possible embarrassment felt by the honored guest at too much praise on his night off. Cleverly, he contrived for a fellow actor to ask:

How look'd he . . . was he tall or short?

Wignell answered:

Why sure I didn't see him. To be sure
As I was looking hard from out the door
I saw a man in regimentals fine,
All lace and glitter, botherum and shine;
And so I look'd at him till all was gone,
And then I found that he was not the one.

At that, Washington burst into a hearty laugh.
Wignell had become the first comedian—but by no means the last—to make a president laugh.

Famous Yankee characters: Bardwell Slote, Rip Van Winkle, Davy Crockett, and Josh Whitcomb.

2

Rubes and Rowdies

Tom Wignell's creation was to be the basis for a long line of Jonathans.

There was Jonathan Norrard of 1792, Jonathan Postfree of 1806, Jonathan from the play *Love and Friendship* of 1809, Jonathan from *The Buck Tails* of 1815, Jonathan Ploughboy in *The Forest Rose* of 1825, Jonathan in *A Trip to Niagara* of 1830, Jonathan in *The Patriot* and *Jonathan Dubikins*, both in 1834. In addition to the characters who carried forward the actual name of Jonathan, there were dozens and dozens of Yankee types based on the original Jonathan concept. They took on other names such as Jedidiah Homebred, Deuteronomy Dutiful, Hiram Dodge, Solomon Swap, Nimrod Wildfire, Solon Shingle, etc. All these characters shared a combination of "Yankee" qualities which made them very popular with their audiences: homespun

George H. "Yankee" Hill and Joshua Silsbee were Yankee imperson-
ators of the period.

awkwardness, cracker-barrel common sense, and a distaste for
fancy manners.

Almost any actor of the period who aspired to prominence,
especially in the field of comedy, was swept into a "Yankee" role
—so popular was the demand. After Wignell there was James H.
Hackett, first native American star; George H. "Yankee" Hill,
who followed in Hackett's footsteps; Joshua Silsbee; Dan Marble;
John E. Owens; and countless others.

Typical of the period's humor was the following from the comedian "Yankee" Hill:

> I once courted a gal by the name of Deb Hawkins. I made it up to
> get married. Well, while we was going up to the deacon's, I stepped
> my foot into a mud puddle, and spattered the mud all over Deb
> Hawkins' new gown, made out of her grandmother's old chintz pet-
> ticoat. Well, when we got to the deacon's, he asked Deb if she would
> take me for her lawful wedded husband. "No," says she, "I shan't do
> no such thing." "What on airth is the reason?" says I. "Why," says
> she, "I've taken a mislikin' to you." Well, it was all up with me then,
> but I give her a string of beads, a few kisses, some other notions, and
> made it all up with her; so we went up to the deacon's a second
> time. I was determined to come up to her this time, so when the
> deacon asked me if I would take her for my lawfully wedded wife,
> says I, "No, I shan't do no such thing." "Why," says Deb, "what on
> airth is the matter?" "Why," says I, "I have taken a mislikin' to *you*

now." Well, there it was all up again, but I gave her a new apron, and a few other little trinkets, and we went up again to get married. We expected then we would be tied so fast that all nature couldn't separate us, and when we asked the deacon if he wouldn't marry us, he said, "No, I shan't dew any sich thing." "Why, what on airth is the reason?" says we. "Why," says he, "I've taken a mislikin' to both of you." Deb burst out crying, the deacon burst out scolding, and I burst out laughing.

So true to life were the impersonations at times that when Joshua Whitcomb, a Yankee character, was taken to Keene, New Hampshire, to present a play, the audience wanted its money back. It couldn't understand being charged admission. Wasn't the character on the stage exactly the same as any number of local citizens who could be seen daily without charge?

Said a representative in protest, "It warn't no acting; it was jest a lot of fellers goin' around and doin' things."

The role of Solon Shingle in a play, *The People's Lawyer*, was known throughout the country. Shingle was an old Yankee farmer, described by the New York *Herald* as the type whom "everyone who has been in that vague place, 'the country,' must remember. He dresses shabbily, but carries fifty dollar bills in his pocket; he makes absurd and ridiculous remarks, but yet has a fund of shrewd sense; he seems very simple and yet is not to be easily outwitted."

Crowds packed the theater nightly when John E. Owens appeared as Shingle, and quotations from the old farmer such as "Why, how do you do?" or "Jesso, jesso," were repeated widely on the streets and in the horse cars and drawing rooms by people who wished to appear witty. Acquaintances would greet each other on the street, "Why, Mr. Winslow, how-do-you-do?" and roar with laughter. In the mid-1800s, Owens, in *The People's Lawyer*, achieved the longest run known till then in any city in America, including New York City.

Scarcely less popular than the Yankee comic character of the period was the character of Mose, the tough citizen of New York's Bowery.

Just as the comic-type Jonathans emerged from actual rural life of the times, so this character reflected life in the big cities, especially New York.

John E. Owens, the great comedian, in one of his comic roles. Owens
(right) is portraying Solon Shingle, one of the most popular Yankee
characters.

The most depraved conditions existed in certain sections of
New York City. The area called the Five Points was located in the
district bounded by Broadway, Canal Street, the Bowery, and
Park Row. It was part of New York's Sixth Ward, sometimes
known as the "Bloody Sixth." Reporting on his visit to this section, Charles Dickens, the English novelist, said: "Here are lanes
and alleys paved with mud knee-deep; underground chambers
where they dance and game; . . . hideous tenements which take
their names from robbery and murder; all that is loathsome,
drooping and decayed is here."

From this congestion, poverty, and misery, sprung one of the
great comic characters of American theater history. In 1849 before a clamorous audience at the old Olympic Theater in New
York, the first presentation of *Mose, the Bow'ry B'hoy* was given
by Francis S. Chanfrau. In this play and in *A Glance at New
York*, which was presented in 1848, Chanfrau presented the
boisterous, comic type of performance for which he became
famous.

As a boy Chanfrau lived in New York's Bowery and was himself one of the rough and ready-to-fight youngsters that he por-
trayed on the stage. In presenting a play reflecting sordid aspects
of city life, even though from a humorous point of view, Chanfrau was concerned that New Yorkers might resent seeing themselves realistically—red shirt, plug hat, pants in boots, cigar-
smoking corrupt politicians and all. The very first line of the

17

A scene from one of F. S. Chanfrau's early "Mose" plays.

play was a statement by Mose: "I'm bound not to run wid der (political) machine any more."

But the response was enthusiastic. For the first time residents of the slums, the underprivileged of the Sixth Ward, began to frequent the theater to see entertainment that reflected their own lives. The politicians came, too. So did the wealthy theatergoers.

True, the newsboys, butcher boys, Bowery B'hoys, and ward heelers did not always behave properly. Once the management at a Chanfrau production had to warn the pit where the cheap seats were located: "Boys, if you misbehave yourselves, I shall raise the prices." Women rarely sat in the pit, where people ate, drank, and spat on the floor. Often in the midst of a performance, rats ran out of holes in the floors into the orchestra.

The Mose series as presented by Chanfrau was filled with reflections of the big-city underworld and the constant battles between the gangs that frequented the Bowery. There was *Mose in California, Mose in a Muss, Mose's Visit to Philadelphia, Mose in China.* So popular did Chanfrau become that at one period he played Mose sketches in two New York theaters and one in Newark, New Jersey, on the same night.

3

Clowns: Whiteface and Black

Two of the greatest clowns of America's early history were Dan Rice and George L. Fox. Rice achieved the height of his popularity in America shortly before the mid-1800s. He started his career aboard a showboat, clowning from port to port in the Midwest.

He was first engaged in 1840 in a traveling puppet show near Reading, Pennsylvania, where he used to exhibit a trained pig. To achieve his comic effects, Rice depended largely on his trained animals, ranging from pigs to mules to horses. The Dan Rice troupe—three performers, a band, and Excelsior, his trick horse— traveled the land entertaining thousands of people. His admirers increased and Rice became known as "the most versatile, spectacular and beloved circus Jester of any country."

During the Civil War, Rice became a friend of President Lincoln and frequently visited him at the White House. There the pair would swap humorous stories until far into the night. Rice is said to have been one of Lincoln's main sources of funny anecdotes. It may have been vice versa. After the Civil War, Rice turned to politics, even seriously seeking the nomination for the presidency against Grant in 1868. Although he received surprising support, he failed to win.

Perhaps even surpassing Rice in his accomplishments was George L. Fox, said to be one of the really funny men of his day. Fox was the first popular American entertainer to follow the ancient tradition of using white pigment on his face as the symbol of the clown.

Fox had amazing control of his facial muscles and was an expert in the comedian's art of grimacing or "mugging." A critic of the period remarked that Fox was not content to please merely by being knocked down many times and jumping over tables and through windows. His muteness and passivity were infinitely more laughable than the bustling antics of other clowns, as was his pose of ignorant simplicity and innocence.

At the old Olympic Theater on Broadway and Bleecker Street in New York, Fox's burlesque of Hamlet was a surefire laugh getter. Laurence Hutton, the critic, wrote:

> He followed the text of Shakespeare closely enough to preserve the plot of the story, and never sank into imbecility or indelicacy. . . .
>
> To see Mr. Fox pacing the platform before the Castle of Elsinore protected against the eager and nipping air of the night by a fur cap and collar, and with mittens and arctic overshoes over the traditional costume of Hamlet; to see the woeful melancholy of his face as he spoke the most absurd of lines; to watch the horror expressed on his countenance when the Ghost appeared; to hear his familiar conversation with that Ghost, and his untraditional profanity when commanded by the Ghost to "swear" . . . was as thoroughly and ridiculously enjoyable as any piece of acting our stage has seen. . . .

Fox burlesqued Hamlet for ten straight weeks. This was tremendously successful. Later in the clown role of Humpty-Dumpty, he played to the New York public more than twelve hundred times, a record for his period.

What Dan Rice and George L. Fox were to clowning, Thomas D. Rice was to the start of blackface minstrel comedy in the 1830s and 1840s. Known as "Daddy" Rice, he achieved fame in entertainment circles almost overnight by blackening his face and doing a comic dance on the stage to the tune of the verse:

> Wheel about, turnabout
> Do just so,
> And everytime I wheel about
> I jump Jim Crow!

Rice was widely imitated. At that time, of course, the words Jim Crow had not taken on the symbolic meaning of racial prejudice

George L. Fox, whiteface clown and pantomimist. He performed for the troops during the Civil War.

which developed later. It was actually the name of an elderly black man, who did a dance similar to that which Rice popularized on the stage. The burnt cork and blackface which he originated have, of course, become commonplace since.

The minstrel character which "Daddy" Rice made popular had its roots in the days of slavery when blacks were forced to dance and sing for their white masters. The adaptation into the minstrel show of the black songs and dances by Northern white imitators

Thomas D. "Daddy" Rice in his early success as a dancer. He helped originate the American minstrel show.

The minstrel show developed into America's sole "native" form of entertainment.

became the sole branch of our dramatic arts to have its beginnings in this country.

The influence of the minstrel extends in many ways to the evolution of comedy. The interlocutor of the minstrel show was really the father of the foil or "straight man" of vaudeville, radio, and television.

Popular as the minstrel show became, it was to have a mature life of no more than twenty-five years in the major entertainment spotlight.

These twenty-five years were destined to see the comic spirit move West with the advancing frontier.

4

Go West, Young Comedian!

There were many stories about the Wild West which might have discouraged an eastern actor from leaving home.

For example, a comedian spread the report that the doorkeeper at a Western theater had to collect the weapons of the audience before admitting the people to the house.

But there were compelling reasons why many actors did go West.

In the more industrialized East, frequent economic crises threw many people out of work. The land to the west gave promise of a freer, better life despite the hardships of frontier living.

Together with covered-wagon migrations went touring theatrical troupes. They came from Boston and New York and went on to Philadelphia, Charleston, Pittsburgh, St. Louis, Salt Lake City, New Orleans, and San Francisco.

It was a serious business, settling a new nation. Perhaps that was one reason why comedians were so welcome, even though their reception was often a rough one.

Mrs. Trollop, a writer visiting from England, was shocked by the audiences which gathered in the new theaters:

Men came into the lower tier or boxes without their coats; and I have seen shirt-sleeves tucked to the shoulders; the spitting was incessant. . . .

The bearing and attitudes of the men is perfectly indescribable; the heels are higher than the head, the entire rear of the person presented to the audience . . . the noises, too, are perpetual, and of the most unpleasant kind; the applause is expressed by cries and thumping with the feet instead of clapping; and when a patriotic fit seizes them, and "Yankee Doodle" is called for, every man seems to think his reputation as a citizen depends on the noise he makes.

Among the young comedians who went West was Joseph Jefferson III, a protege of "Daddy" Rice. The young Jefferson, a laughmaker of distinction, headed west on a barnstorming trip to Chicago, then on to Springfield, Illinois.

When Jefferson and his company reached Springfield, they discovered that a religious revival was in progress. The fathers of the church not only launched forth against the theater in sermons, but had taken political measures to have a new law passed, using taxation to virtually outlaw theatrical presentations of any kind.

This created a difficult situation for the comedians and for the theater managers who had invested considerable sums in founding a theater in the city. Furthermore, the town was full of people at this time, and a guaranteed audience was on hand. But the action against performing was not a matter to be treated lightly. As Mr. Jefferson himself described it:

In the midst of our trouble a young lawyer called on the managers. He had heard of the injustice and offered, if they would place the matter in his hands, to have the license taken off, declaring that he only desired to see fair play, and he would accept no fee whether he failed or succeeded.

The case was brought up before the council. The young lawyer began his harangue. He handled the subject with tact, skill and humor, tracing the history of the drama from the time when Thespis acted in a cart to the stage of today. He illustrated his speech with a number of anecdotes, and kept the council in a roar of laughter; his good humor prevailed and the exorbitant tax was taken off.

This young lawyer was very popular in Springfield, and was honored and beloved by all who knew him, and after the time of which I write he held rather an important position in the government of the United States.

This was not the only occasion on which Abraham Lincoln expressed his interest in the subject of the theater.

Lincoln came a long way from the time when, as a young law-

Whereas the sedate audiences that had frequented the theater were mostly limited to well-to-do groups, the newly developing comedy attracted rough-and-ready sections of the population, not as concerned about manners as about having a thoroughly good time.

yer, he had helped Joseph Jefferson win the right to present a play in Springfield. So did the young comedian. But Joseph Jefferson's rise had not been easy. Somehow theater managers refused to recognize him as a comedian.

"Oh, you are the new young comedian, eh?" was the way one manager greeted me.

"But you do not look like a comedian," he said to me. "You have a serious melancholy expression; you look more like an undertaker."

Jefferson's special talents as described by his friend William Winter in the 1850s and 1860s included his ability "to touch, in his true and delicate manner, the springs of tears and laughter. . . ."

Jefferson's acting has always been remarkable for tenderness of heart . . . and for the spontaneous drollery, the condition of being an amusing person, which comes by nature, and which cannot be taught. . . . His crowning excellence as a comedian is, that he . . . does not stop at being a photographic copyist of the eccentric, the rustic, the ludicrous and the grotesque. . . . The level upon which he treads is that of humanity, in its laughable, mournful admixture of weakness, suffering, patience, amiability, despondency, hope and endeavor. . . .

Jefferson's first major comic role was that of Asa Trenchard in the play *Our American Cousin* which was presented for the first time in 1858. The play ran 140 consecutive nights.

James H. Hackett in his role as Falstaff, which attracted the commendation of President Lincoln. Hackett was one of the first native American theatrical stars and was a master of mimicry. Hackett's early reputation was gained from his "Yankee" roles.

It was, however, as Rip in the play *Rip Van Winkle* that Jefferson earned his great reputation. Seeing Jefferson perform, John Drew, the noted actor, exclaimed: "Gentlemen, I have had a very pleasant experience; I have seen a part played as well as it could be."

One incident relating to Jefferson and the death of a fellow comedian, George Holland, is revealing. When Holland died, the family asked Jefferson to call upon the pastor of a nearby church and ask him to officiate at the service. Jefferson went to the minister and explained that they wished to have arrangements made for the time and place of the funeral. When the minister learned that Mr. Holland had been an actor, he refused point-blank to perform the funeral rites. Jefferson said, recalling the incident:

> I rose to leave the room with a mortification that I cannot remember to have felt before or since. I paused at the door and said:
> "Well, sir, in this dilemma is there no other church to which you can direct me from which my friend can be buried?"
> He replied that, "There is a little church around the corner" where I might get it done; to which I answered:
> "Then God bless the little church around the corner," so I left the house.

The incident somehow got into the newspapers and brought a storm of protest. The fact that the Church of the Transfiguration (The Little Church Around the Corner) willingly accepted the funeral and that Holland was buried in a quiet ceremony did not for a moment bury the incident itself.

On the contrary, various newspapers made the subject front-page news and pulled forth nationwide editorial discussion. He was recognized, too, as having done more than anyone to elevate the social and intellectual standing of the actor and the stage.

Nor did the incident stop with the critical comment of the press. On January 19, 1871, every New York theater opened its doors for a benefit for the Holland family. Actors, singers, acrobats, dancers, and comedians volunteered their services as a loving testimony to George Holland.

There were similar testimonials in support of The Little Church Around the Corner and for the benefit of Holland's widow and children in Brooklyn, San Francisco, Boston, Vicksburg, Washington, D.C., and elsewhere.

Joseph Jefferson in one of his most popular roles, that of Asa Trenchard in Our American Cousin.

The burial of George Holland actually marked more than the passing of a comedian. It marked the end of an era. While Jefferson himself lived on to continue his portrayal of Rip Van Winkle and even to participate in an early motion picture, the times were changing.

A new type of comedian was in the wings of the American theater, eager to take the spotlight. He was not to be in the image of a Holland or a Jefferson. Rather he was to revert to a crude type of Jonathan. Music-hall and vaudeville comedy was about to be born and Tony Pastor was the father.

5

Low Comedy and the Elegant Eighties

The country was changing, its audiences were changing, and the comedy needs were changing, too. The new comedy was no longer to be found in the theater of Jefferson and Hackett, popular as it remained. The music halls, the beer halls, the minstrel shows, and the broad comedy of burlesque were to bring forth the variety or vaudeville show.

Before the Civil War, a young man by the name of Tony Pastor found employment in the circus and became a clown. He tumbled with the acrobats and danced in the minstrel shows. In 1860 he became a comic vocalist in a Broadway music hall and then opened up his own place, a cheap nightclub, offering beer, wine, liquor, and hostesses.

Tony Pastor had an instinct for recognizing entertainment talent. He conceived the idea of organizing a road show with plenty of comedy in it. It was a success from the outset. He increased his tours and played every prominent town on the map. In 1881 Pastor opened his 14th Street Theater in the Tammany Hall Building in New York. It was something new: a "variety show" with something for everyone, a show children could take their parents to. Under Tony's tutelage, many a future headliner learned the beginnings of the acting profession, especially comedy.

While Pastor was planting the seeds of future vaudeville, a man by the name of Michael B. Leavitt was doing the same for burlesque. Burlesque was a variety show with short skits, bawdy humor, and slapstick comedy. Leavitt was a hard-headed and unsentimental gentleman, a former child actor, and a manager of a troupe of minstrel and variety performers in the early days. It was Leavitt who developed the burlesque show of modern times.

To the names of Pastor and Leavitt was to be added a third, Benjamin Franklin Keith, to whom credit goes for founding a traveling circuit for vaudeville. Having received his start in a dime museum as a circus man, in 1883 Keith broke with his partner and bought the Bijou Theater in Boston where his ingenuity helped to invent the modern form of vaudeville.

Keith had the idea that a continuous show of entertainment would attract people. The program would consist of a number of specialty acts such as singing, dancing, comic acts, magicians, acrobats, jugglers, and performing animals. One Sunday morning, he advertised the continuous performance idea in the Boston newspapers, stating: "Come when you please, stay as long as you like." The idea was revolutionary—but it worked. Admission was a dime in Boston's Bijou, and "for five cents more one could obtain a chair."

Some of Keith's friends thought he was heading for certain trouble if he let people stay as long as they liked. The turnover, they feared, would be astonishingly small. Of course, P. T. Barnum, the circus king, had pretty much the same problem. He had solved it by putting up a sign which read THIS WAY TO THE EGRESS. Many of his customers thought that this was some kind of strange animal or bird and, imagine their surprise when, upon walking through the door, they found themselves out on the street.

Keith's variety—or vaudeville—show attracted greater and greater attention. The idea was extended from Boston to Providence to Philadelphia and eventually to New York. Keith took over the Union Square Theater in New York, which was then the home of the legitimate stage. His wife was personally interested in removing the stigma of doubtful morality which surrounded the variety shows and music-hall entertainment. As the Keith Circuit grew, every theater carried a sign on its bulletin board backstage that read:

NOTICE TO PERFORMERS

Don't say "slob" or "son of gun" or "Holy gee" on the stage unless you want to be cancelled peremptorily. Do not address anyone in

A comic dancer of the turn of the century era.

the audience in any manner. If you have not the ability to entertain Mr. Keith's audiences without risk of offending them, do the
best you can. Lack of talent will be less open to censure than would
be an insult to a patron. If you are in doubt as to the character of
your act, consult the local manager before you go on stage, for if
you are guilty of uttering anything sacrilegious or even suggestive,
you will be immediately closed and will never again be allowed in
a theater where Mr. Keith is in authority.

Keith teamed up with B. F. Albee, and the Keith-Albee enter-
prises spread their influence throughout the developing nation.

The years from 1877 to 1882 marked the end of the era of the
great local theater companies and the start of an era of traveling
companies. Shakespeare and the traditional repertoire were fading
into the background. Musical comedy was taking the public by
storm. New names, particularly the names of comedians, were
gaining popularity.

Most of the early variety comedy was racial or national, reflecting migration waves which brought Irish, Italian, German, Eastern European, and Jewish people to these shores in large numbers.
Comedy was crude. People laughed at such side-splitters as these:

Straight Man: If I didn't have this hangout here I don't know what
I'd do. (Inevitable knock.) Come in. (Enter comic.)

Comic: Good mawnin'. I just stopped in for some information.

Straight: I'll try to accommodate you. What is it?

Comic: What time does the three o'clock train go out?

Straight: The three o'clock train? Why, it goes out exactly sixty minutes past two o'clock.

Comic: That's funny. The man at the station told me it went out exactly sixty minutes before four o'clock.

Straight: Well, you won't miss your train, anyway.

Comic: No. Well, I'm much obliged. (Exits.)

Rules and regulations of the famous Wallack's Theatre of the later 1800s were hard on comedians. Ad libbing was penalized, as point six indicates.

WALLACK'S TH

...

1. Gentlemen, at the time of rehearsal of performance, are not to wear their hats in the Green Room, or talk vociferously. The Green Room is a place appropriated for the quiet and regular meeting of the company, who are to be called thence, *and thence only*, by the call boy, to attend on the stage. The Manager is not to be applied to in that place, on any matter of business, or with any personal complaint. For a breach of any part of this article, fifty cents will be forfeited.

2. The call for all rehearsals will be put up by the Prompter between the play and farce, or earlier, on evenings of performance. No plea that such call was not seen will be received. All rehearsals must be attended. For absence from each scene, a fine of twenty-five cents; whole rehearsal, five dollars.

3. Any person appearing intoxicated on the stage shall forfeit a week's salary, and be liable to be discharged.

4. For making stage wait—fine, one dollar.

5. A Performer rehearsing from a book or part at the last rehearsal of a new piece, and after proper time given ready, forfeits one dollar.

6. A Performer introducing his own language or improper jests not in the author, or swearing in his part, shall forfeit one dollar.

7. A Performer refusing a part allotted him or her, by the Manager, will forfeit his or her salary during the run of the piece, and on any night of it

10. In all
to himself the
during the ab

11. No per
the audience,
Any violation
forfeiture of
Manager.

12. No Pr
permitted to
to the Theatr
under the pen

13. Every
provide him
stockings, wi
may be appro
is wearing.
the whole of it

14. The reg
ances will app

15. Ladies
permit them i

16. Ladies
bring children
required in th

17. It is pa
gentleman wil
ive places of

Straight: Curious sort of chap. (Picks up banjo and strums quietly as comic reenters.)

Comic: Excuse me, which is the other side of the street?

Straight: Why, the other side of the street is just across the way.

Comic: That's funny. I asked the fellow across the street and he said it was over here.

Straight: Well, you can't depend on everything you hear.

Comic: No, that's so.

At about this period, one of the most celebrated teams in the history of the American theater became a New York sensation. It was the team of Edward Harrigan and Tony Hart, whose popularity knew no equal. The pair's shrewd realism and sympathetic understanding of racial and national values brought them a vast following.

Harrigan's plays had their inception as vaudeville sketches consisting of songs and dialogue. Out of these grew his full-length plays centering around the New York Irish. For fourteen years Harrigan and Hart were a much-esteemed and enormously successful team. To many out-of-towners Harrigan and Hart were a

Lotta Crabtree was a fabulous figure of the early American stage. One of the few comediennes with a national following, Lotta started on the West Coast as a red-headed child actress who could dance, sing, and play the banjo. She became a national favorite and died the richest actress in America.

Lotta is the only known comedienne in the nation's history whose memory is marked by a public fountain. "Lotta's Fountain"— donated by the wealthy actress to the city of San Francisco in 1875—is located at the intersection of Kearny, Market, and Geary streets.

New York landmark equal in stature to Broadway. "A visit to New York would be as incomplete to the countryman if he did not see Harrigan and Hart, as if he had by some strange mistake missed going to Central Park," declared one New England guidebook in the eighties.

Harrigan and Hart complemented each other, or as the Boston *Traveler* stated, "Hart could play all the parts seven Harrigans could write and Harrigan could write what seven Harts could play." Harrigan was a prolific writer. In addition to some eighty or ninety sketches that he wrote while working in variety theaters as a young actor, he was the author of some thirty-five full-length plays. Not only this, but Harrigan went on to act in his own plays, sing his own songs, and finally ended up by producing, financing, and directing them himself. He even wrote the text for his own programs. Harrigan was sometimes characterized as "the Dickens of America." Harrigan and Hart appealed not so much to the upper-class theatergoers of New York, but to the inhabitants of the slums, the newsboys, the flower girls, the barbers, the butchers, the Bowery toughs and the South Street sailors, and the disreputable folks who made up the bulk of the followers of Chanfrau and his Bowery-B'hoy productions of years before. The pair also attracted the politicians of New York, even though the team would engage in the sharpest satire against corrupt practices of the day. The gossipy weekly, *Town Topics*, reported in 1886 after attending a performance of the *O'Reagans*:

> A brutal alderman sat beside me and roared when Mr. Wild (Harrigan) remarked with all his power that the politicians had stolen all the stars from the American flag and were now wearing the stripes. The brutal alderman did not believe him, of course, but it might be that if anyone in life had passed this same jest to him, he would probably have committed homicide or mayhem. This is the

Harrigan and Hart comprised the most famous comedy team of their day. They continued the rough-and-tumble type of humor begun by Chanfrau many years before. A visit to New York was incomplete until you had seen a Harrigan and Hart show. Here, they are in costume. Hart frequently played the role of a woman.

soul of Harrigan's peculiar talent. He sees the life he is a part of and translates it as a commentator, rather than as a critic.

For some twenty years Harrigan and Hart reigned over the New York theater. On one occasion when Harrigan and Hart threatened to separate, such a hue and cry was raised that a special committee of politicians called upon New York's mayor, William R. Grace, and asked him as a civic contribution to offer his good services in an attempt to heal the breach. The Mayor dutifully tried and got nowhere. After the rift, both actors went their own ways, but neither was able to achieve anything approaching their previous accomplishments.

The comedy team which followed closely upon the heels of Harrigan and Hart, Jim McIntyre and Tom Heath, owed much to the pioneering work of those two men. But theirs was a blackface act. They started in 1874 and continued until the 1930s. McIntyre and Heath were not slapstick comedians, but presented fine characterizations and drew real belly laughs. They became the oldest two-man act in vaudeville. Strangely enough, while the team remained intact until the thirties, offstage the men seldom spoke to each other and even lived in different hotels when possible.

Tom Heath was the straight man while Jim McIntyre played the comic. Heath assumed the role of the smaller and downtrodden black man while Tom Heath was the overbumptious "Hennery." On the stage, McIntyre and Heath were so sure of each other that if one sprang a new joke, he knew that the other would come right back quick as a flash with a funny answer. People who had seen them do the same scene two nights in succession noted that the two versions might be entirely different.

"In all comedy teams," stated McIntyre, "there are the straight actor and the comedian. The former feeds the lines to the comedian so the latter can get off the jokes that bring the laughs. We have never worked that way. Heath is the straight man and I am the comedian. But the way we do things is this: Heath says something that gives me a chance to make a joke that gets a laugh; but my joke always gives him a chance to come back with an answer that gets another laugh."

"You might say that we're selling laughs," stated Heath. "If Jim can sell an extra one, I get half the proceeds. If I can sell an

James McIntyre and Thomas Heath were another successful blackface team. They worked together for over fifty years. When McIntyre died in 1937, he was followed to grave one year later by his partner.

extra one, Jim gets half the proceeds. We never forgot that we are financially interested in each other's work. That's the way men in any kind of business ought to feel."

Top women comedians were rare in the theater of the 1880s. But there was no more lovable comic character in the country than May Irwin, a product of Tony Pastor's variety shows and probably the most beloved woman of her era.

Theatre Magazine described Miss Irwin as "the funniest stage woman in America," and in an interview asked her how she got that way. Miss Irwin answered:

Humor is spontaneous. It is born with one or it is not. It cannot be acquired and it cannot be forced. . . . I often receive letters from magazines asking me to write on the humorous side of this or that. Many times I sit, my fountain pen clutched in my hand, my features tense as a tragedian's and nothing happens. . . .

I can't, that's all. Sometimes it is quite otherwise. The subject . . . is comprised in the radius of my interests. . . .

To me humor is unanalyzable. It comes or it does not. It is as mysterious as and less controllable than electricity. That which is called the comic mind seizes upon the funny points in a play and makes the most of them.

If Harrigan was versatile and appealed to vast numbers of comedy-hungry people, a brash young man who was born and raised

Fred Stone and David Montgomery were a comedy team of unique talent. The pair is shown in a scene from The Wizard of Oz.

in the shadow of the theater was ready to pick up where Harrigan and Hart left off. His name was George M. Cohan, the youngest of the Cohan family of four, a well-known vaudeville act.

Swift-moving and vigorous, Cohan moved into the theatrical world at the turn of the century like a whirling tornado. He soon had the nation singing his tunes and laughing at his jokes. Before he ended his career (although it came late), he was awarded the Congressional Medal of Honor by President Franklin D. Roosevelt for writing two of the nation's most popular song hits: "Over There" and "A Grand Old Flag."

From the start, Cohan used his own brand of breeziness and concocted a series of fast-moving plays, plays which gave the impression of a great machine shooting out characters, choruses, songs, and dances with the rapidity of a machine gun.

Known as a song-and-dance man, Cohan almost singlehandedly, out of the corner of his mouth, changed the face of musical comedy and introduced into the theater a flag-waving content which had no equal short of a Fourth of July parade. He even claimed the Fourth of July as his birthday.

But in a sense, Cohan carried on the traditional Yankee character which had its start in the Jonathan of the earlier days. *Theatre*

George M. Cohan, the great song-and-dance man, made frequent use of patriotic themes in his plays. A plaque at his birthplace in Providence, Rhode Island, set his birthday characteristically as July 4th. A peek at his birth certificate, however, shows the date as July 3rd.

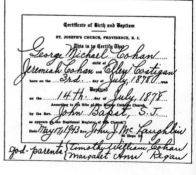

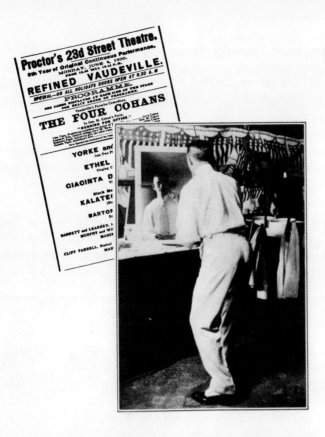

George M. Cohan getting ready for the opening curtain.

Magazine stated:

> To a large part of the public Cohan represents the restless Ameri-
> can spirit, the cheeky go-aheadness of the hustling Yankee. All the
> time he is on the stage he is in motion. His hat worn jauntily on
> one side of his head, his face screwed up into a perpetual grin, his
> legs never still for a moment, coming in with the skit that soon
> develops into a hilarious dance, singing his own songs with a nasal
> drawl and forever waving a flag.

Eddie Foy, in the same period, was a genial and capable funny
man. His rise is the story of a bootblack who spent his spare time
practicing dancing, singing, and acrobatics.

He won a warm spot in the hearts of the American people.
Graduating from minstrel shows and beer halls, he turned to vaudeville and musical comedy, where he was a star for thirty years.

Before he ended his career, he had accumulated a huge following of admirers and enough of his own children (seven) to present an entire family act.

Foy's humor was gentle and nonaggressive, but the same cannot be said for two young men—one tall and one short—who entered the theater when they were nine years old and did not leave it until they had become world-famous. Their career spanned a period from the beginnings of vaudeville to the coming of radio and motion pictures. They were the famous comedy team of Joe Weber and Lew Fields. From their very start in the early eighties, as Weber himself said, "All the public wanted to see was Fields knock the hell out of me."

Eddie Foy, Comedian, the Real Hero of the Great Fire Tragedy

Actor First Tried to Quiet Audience, Then Saw That Members of His Company Got Out Safely.

In 1903, Eddie Foy became a national hero as a result of his courage in the Iroquois Theater fire in Chicago. Almost six hundred men, women, and children lost their lives. Attired in his clown costume, Foy sought to reassure the terrified audience and was among the last to leave the doomed theater alive. Above, an account of the fire and a copy of the theater program which described the theater as "absolutely fireproof."

Fields said, "I don't know why it was, but the audience always seemed to have a grudge against him," (meaning Joe Weber). Like so many of their predecessors since the days of Thomas "Daddy" Rice, Weber and Fields started in their careers as black-face comedians. But to win a position in the theater world they showed a maximum flexibility. They composed their lyrics so that they could change them to fit whatever opportunity happened to arise. "Here we are, an Irish pair," they sang, or when another

43

type of comedian was needed, they changed the words to, "Here we are, a German pair." From the earliest days the Weber and Fields type of humor was rough-and-tumble and included murdering the English language as well as almost murdering each other.

Their humor, while it may be dated now, was hilarious then:

"Who is that lady I saw you with last night?" asked Weber.

"She ain't no lady, she's my wife," answered Fields while the audience roared. The echoes of that one still persist in the land.

Another typical Weber and Fields exchange went like this:

MIKE: I am delightfulness to meet you.

MYER: Der disgust is all mine.

MIKE: I receivedidid a letter from mein goil, but I don't know how to writteninin her back.

MYER: Writteninin her back! Such an edumuncation you got it? Writteninin her back! You mean rotteninin her back. How can you answer her ven you don't know how to write?

MIKE: Dot makes no nefer mind. She don't know how to read.

MYER: If you luf her, vy don't you send her some poultry?

MIKE: She don't need no poultry; her father is a butcher.

MYER: I mean luf voids like Romeo and Chuliet talks.
If you luf you like I luf me
No knife can cut us togedder.

MIKE: I don't like dot.

MYER: Vell, vot do you vant to say to her?

MIKE: I don't vant you to know vat I'm saying to her. All I vant you to do is tell me vot to put in her letter.

MYER: Such foolishness you are! If I don't tell you vot to say, how vill you know vot to write if she don't know how to read?

MIKE: I don't vant nobody to know vot I'm writteninin to her.

MYER: You don't vant anyone to know vot you are rotteninin?

MIKE: No.

MYER: Then send her a postal card.

MIKE: Send her a postal card? If I do she'll think I don't care two cendts for her.

MYER: Are you going to marry her?

MIKE: In two days I vill be a murdered man.

MYER: Vot?

MIKE: I mean a married man.

MYER: I hope you vill always look back upon der presendt moment as der habbiest moment uff your life.

MIKE: But I aind't married yet.

MYER: I know it, und furdermore, upon dis suspicious occasion, I also vish to express to you—charges collect—my uppermost depreciation of der dishonor you haf informed upon me in making me your bridesmaid.

MIKE: Der insuldt is all mein.

Although Weber and Fields may appear today to be merely another slapstick team, actually they were innovators of the most influential kind. Until they came upon the scene, the usual comedy was either pure slapstick, or mere gag patter. Weber and Fields were among the first to base their comedy on topics of the day, combining slapstick with sharp social satire. The theater was not the same after they were finished with it.

They were innovators in many other ways. They would have nothing to do with vulgarity. Their shows were clean and they boasted of this. Weber and Fields were among the first to introduce the notion of women attending theatrical productions. The drinking and smoking male audience, rather than the performance itself, was a barrier to women's attendance at the theater. Women complained that men monopolized the theater.

Once when playing at Jim Fennessey's People's Theater in Cincinnati, Fields suggested to Colonel Fennessey that one night a week be set aside when smoking and drinking be banned and women admitted. Fennessey was aghast. "Let sleeping dogs lie, son," he said pleadingly, "Let 'em in here once and they'll be pushing in regular the first thing you know and driving the boys away. A man likes to have some place where he can get away from petticoats."

But Fields insisted and finally the Colonel reluctantly agreed that "we might reserve the boxes for them some night and let a few in through the stage door." But Weber and Fields were not satisfied. "Why not do the thing up brown and get it talked about?" they asked. "Get out a lot of dodgers announcing Friday as 'Ladies' Night'; no smoking, no drinking and a cut flower presented to every lady present. Give the old house a thorough scrubbing and fill your lobby with flowers. Try it once." Fennessey grunted, "It's a crazy idea and against my better judgment, but have your own way."

Friday came and by evening the theater was gleamingly clean. The ladies were admitted, and from that time on, the theater was never again to recapture its former bachelor status. "Ladies' Night" became a Cincinnati institution and Weber and Fields had done it.

So well associated were the names of Weber and Fields that America looked upon them interchangeably, but after many years, the partners split one night with the final performance of the show *Whoop-dee-doo*.

The breakup became the subject of national discussion, was heralded in all the papers, and was thought to be a national catastrophe.

Few teams of comedians in the history of the theater achieved the place in the hearts of so many people as the team of Weber and Fields in their prime. The theater was somehow not the same after the pair separated.

Significantly, Lew Fields kept the Weber and Fields Theater open for several years after the split, taking into temporary partnership a young man from Chicago who seemed to have an eye for showmanship and women—especially women.

His name was Florenz Ziegfeld.

Weber and Fields were more than a great comedy combination. They were innovators. They combined hastily improvised comedy, sentimental and witty songs, acrobatics, slapstick, dialect stories, parodies, and burlesques.

6

From Follies to Flickers

When Weber and Fields split, the dapper young man with a flair for showmanship who stepped into the breach was to glorify more chorus girls and comedians than any producer up to his time—or since.

Florenz Ziegfeld created a new form of American theatrical presentation which he labeled the *Ziegfeld Follies*. His *Follies* were eye-filling spectacles which raided musical comedy and vaudeville for beautiful women and funny laughmakers. The first *Ziegfeld Follies* opened in 1907.

In the name of glorifying the American girl, Ziegfeld stripped her of her clothes and had her walk around the stage with a huge fan and a haughty look. Ziegfeld's formula for his new type of revue was simple: first, beautiful girls; second, good comedians; and third, lush backgrounds.

Ziegfeld was no judge of comedy, nor did he profess to be, but his *Follies* were the setting for some of the greatest comic genius in the history of the American theater.

Ziegfeld rarely smiled at his comedians, although in the years that the *Ziegfeld Follies* were popular, from 1907 to 1931, he featured such fun makers as Leon Errol, Bert Williams, Fanny Brice, George Bickell, Frank Tinney, Ed Wynn, W. C. Fields, Nat Wills, Eddie Cantor, Will Rogers, Ed Gallagher and Al Shean, Ray Dooley, Bert Wheeler, and Willie Howard.

Ziegfeld owed much to American burlesque. As the critic

George Jean Nathan said at the time:

> The loudest and most popular laughter in the American theatres of today is provoked by humor that has been graduated from burlesque . . . the leading comedians of a dozen or more shows of uniformly high prosperity throughout the country have come to the more urgent stage from burlesque, and have brought their wheezes with them.

Among the most popular comedians whom the *Ziegfeld Follies* brought forward was Bert Williams. He had a unique way of rendering songs: injecting his talk between rests and catching up with the melodic phrase after he had let it get a head start.

Williams was the first black entertainer since the early nineties to appear in an all-white show before Southern audiences. He was a natural-born mimic as well as a singer and dancer. Because he was lighter-skinned, he had to use the traditional burnt cork makeup when on stage.

Discussing his comedy role, Williams told a friend, "Speaking of new laughs, they are only younger than the old ones, and not quite so sincere. Did you ever hear of the origin of Joe Miller's joke book? You know, it was found in the library of Noah's Ark."

Before entering the *Follies*, Williams achieved national prominence as a comedian and dancer in combination with George Walker. His fame even spread abroad, and when he was at the Shaftsebury Theatre in London, Williams was invited to attend a lawn party at Buckingham Palace to entertain the guests at a birthday party of King Edward VII. It was on this occasion that Williams was able to teach the king the elements of the American Cake Walk, a dance popular at home.

Williams was the hit of the *Follies* during the early years. "I'm just out here to give the gals time to change," he would tell the audience.

One of the funniest scenes people remember from the *Follies* featured the comedian, Leon Errol, who made a specialty of imitating a typical drunk whether it was a sailor, a husband, a cowboy, or even Louis XIV.

Errol's stock in trade was his own type of stagger dancing which defied the laws of equilibrium. Buckling his rubbery legs,

According to Eddie Cantor, "Bert Williams was one of the finest artists. . . . His knack for rhythmic timing . . . has never been excelled."

he looked as if he would not be able to stand a moment longer, careening from one end of the stage to the other.

One of the greatest comic acts of all times was this combination of Bert Williams and Leon Errol. In the *Follies* of 1911, the pair took part in a skit, "Upper and Lower Level." The scene was in New York's Grand Central Station and Williams would play the part of a redcap while Errol was a Major Waterbrush.

The act started with precisely four written lines and then Williams and Errol would carry on, ad libbing, improvising, creating such hilarity through their pantomiming and spontaneous humor that an act which was to last but a few minutes stretched to almost half an hour.

According to the report, the manager wired Ziegfeld, who was in Chicago at the time, that the pair threatened to disorganize the entire show. Ziegfeld wired back curtly to curb them. But the situation was beyond the control of the manager.

When Ziegfeld returned East, he had every intention of knocking the troublesome act from the *Follies* repertoire. But as he stood in the rear of the theater watching the pair, he was unable to restrain his laughter. Williams and Errol stayed.

During his lifetime, Williams was called "The Son of Laughter" and "King of Comedy." W. C. Fields, himself a comic actor of the

Follies, thought Williams "the funniest man I ever saw and the saddest man I ever saw. I often wonder whether other people sensed what I did in him—a deep undercurrent of pathos."

Eddie Cantor, who made a name for himself as a comedian in the *Follies,* too, says:

> Bert Williams was not only a great comic, but extremely human and possessed of fine sensibilities. It happened in St. Louis that he walked up to a bar and asked for gin.
>
> The bartender, reluctant to serve a Negro, said, "I'll give you gin, but it's fifty dollars a glass."
>
> Bert Williams quietly took out his billfold and produced a $500 bill.
>
> "Give me ten of them," he said.

Booker T. Washington, the famous black educator, once said: "Bert Williams has done more for the race than I have. He has smiled his way into people's hearts. I have been obliged to *fight* my way."

Another of Ziegfeld's great comic characters was Fanny Brice, who fought her way upward from amateur-night contests to become one of the great comediennes in American theatrical history.

Fanny was one of the few girls Ziegfeld hired for reasons other than beauty. What Fanny lacked by Ziegfeld's standards, however, she made up in her quick mind, expressive eyes, and comic spirit. Fanny had a sense of caricature which was nothing short of brilliant. She could lampoon anyone from a fan dancer to an evangelist. Fanny Brice was in almost every *Follies* from 1910 to 1923. When the *Ziegfeld Midnight Frolic* started on the Amsterdam Roof, Fanny was in that. She would play the regular *Follies,* then go upstairs with other selected members of the cast to do the *Frolic.*

Many years later, she starred in a radio program, "Ziegfeld Follies on the Air," and in the movie, *The Great Ziegfeld.* When *The Ziegfeld Follies* was made as a picture, Fanny participated. And when the Shuberts revived the *Follies,* shortly after Ziegfeld died, Fanny headed the cast.

Fanny had an assortment of grotesque expressions which she used interchangeably. Some thought Fanny's success was due to

Fanny Brice was one of the few comediennes to challenge the supremacy of the men in winning laughs.

the way she contrasted with the beauties whom Ziegfeld carefully collected for his chorus. But Fanny was funny when she was appearing by herself, whether on the radio as "Baby Snooks," in the motion picture, or in a musical revue or a *Ziegfeld Follies*.

On the subject of comedy, Fanny would say:

You get your first laugh—boom! you're going. You lose yourself, you become whatever it is they're laughing at, but it isn't you. Anytime I ever did any kind of dance, don't you think that in my heart, as I am making them laugh, that I don't want them to say: "She's really so graceful"?

If you're a comic you have to be nice. And the audience has to like you. You have to have a softness about you, because if you do comedy and you are harsh, there is something offensive about it. Also you must set up your audience for the laugh you are working for. So you go along and everything is fine, like any other act, and then —boom! you give it to them. Like there is a beautiful painting of a woman and you paint a mustache on her.

While Ziegfeld was not an enthusiast for comedians, there was one whom he appreciated. He rarely missed an opportunity to watch Will Rogers work. "You know," Ziegfeld once said, "I'm not supposed to have a very quick sense of humor. . . . But this Rogers, I never miss him if I can help it, though you'd be surprised at

53

Bobby Clark was another Follies *comedian. The combination of Clark and Paul McCullough (left) was one of the more successful comedy partnerships.*

how many of my expensive comics I've run out on and locked myself in my office when they were on the stage."

Rogers seldom rehearsed with the *Follies*. He would follow a policy of studying the current news, going over it carefully prior to his performance. It was for this reason that his performances were of as great interest to his fellow entertainers as to the audience.

One of Rogers' earliest jokes from the stage took place when he was twirling a rope in vaudeville. During a lull, he remarked carelessly to the audience: "Swingin' a rope's all right—if your neck ain't in it."

The audience was taken by surprise by his casual comment and roared with laughter. Following the performance, Rogers was abashed and vowed never to speak again, but to carry on his roping act completely in silence. However, his fellow entertainers convinced him that he should employ, as part of his roping act, some of the jokes and humorous anecdotes that he was forever using when off the stage. It was this combination of roping and joking that won him an appearance before Ziegfeld.

In those early days Rogers was far from confident that he would have sufficient gags to keep his audience laughing. He went so far as to keep in his back pocket a little memorandum, which he entitled "Gags for Missing the Horse's Nose," in which he had listed eight little reminders of funny things to say. He found, however, that by studying the newspapers he was able to find enough humorous situations to keep him well supplied. Soon he had mastered the technique of maintaining a sufficient reservoir of humorous sayings to keep him in good supply during his entire routine.

Will Rogers was frequently quoted on the floor of Congress. However, on one occasion he was sharply criticized.

When a gentleman quoted me on the floor of Congress the other day (he reported), another member took exception and said he objected to the remarks of a Professional Joke Maker going into the Congressional Record.

Now can you beat that for jealousy among people in the same line? Calling me a Professional Joke Maker! He is right about everything but the Professional. *They* are the Professional Joke Makers. Read some of the Bills that they have passed, if you think they warn't Joke Makers. I could study all my life and not think up half the amount of funny things they can think of in one Session of Congress. Besides, my jokes don't do anybody any harm. You don't have to pay any attention to them. But every one of the jokes these Birds make is a *Law* and hurts somebody (generally everybody).

"Joke Maker"! He couldn't have coined a better term for Congress

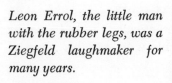

Leon Errol, the little man with the rubber legs, was a Ziegfeld laughmaker for many years.

if he had been inspired. But I object to being called a Professional. I am an Amateur beside them. If I had that Guy's unconscious Humor, Ziegfeld couldn't afford to pay me I would be so funny.

Rogers' major emphasis was on politics, and he was able to present his observations in quick and sure and homely phrases. A growing number of people looked upon Rogers as sort of an ideal American statesman, and he was seriously suggested for every office including that of president.

"There's already too many comedians in Washington," he replied laughing. "Competition would be too keen for me."

Nothing seemed to faze Rogers. His good humor and natural simplicity seemed to remove the barb of sharpness from his jokes. On one occasion he was the main speaker at a convention of bankers. He started off his remarks by saying: "You're as fine a group of men as ever foreclosed on a widow. I am glad to be with you Shylocks."

Will Rogers was one of the most versatile of all American comedians. Not only was he an outstanding star in vaudeville and in the *Follies*, but he doubled for Fred Stone, his close friend, in a musical revue when Stone broke his legs in an accident.

Altogether Rogers made about twenty-four silent films and a number of motion pictures of the talkie variety. Discussing his advent into the movies, Rogers commented, "Well, there was a move on foot for making fewer and worse pictures, so they hired me."

Writing from Hollywood on how he broke into the movies, Rogers said:

Out here in Hollywood they say you're not a success unless you owe $50,000 to somebody, have five cars, can develop temperament without notice or reason at all, and been mixed up in four divorce cases and two breach of promise cases.

Well, as a success in Hollywood, I'm a rank failure and I guess I'm too old to teach new tricks and besides I'm pretty well off domestically speaking and ain't yearnin' for a change.

And it was true. As his close friend Marie Dressler, a comedienne in her own right, said, "He is practically the only public figure I know who has kept his hair, his wife, and his sense of humor twenty-five years."

There is only one statue of a comedian in Statuary Hall in the nation's Capitol. It is of Will Rogers. Others of the seventy-five statues include Sam Adams, John Calhoun, George Washington, Daniel Webster, and Roger Williams. The statue of Rogers is the only one showing pants in need of pressing.

One of Will Rogers' comedian teammates in several of the *Ziegfeld Follies* was the former juggler and unique comedian, W. C. Fields. Outside of being on the same payroll, Will Rogers and Fields had very little in common although both were comedians of major stature.

William Claud Dukinfield, as W. C. Fields was named at birth, was one of a number of jugglers turned comedian, a list which includes Fred Allen, Eddie Cantor, and Jimmy Savo. Fields described himself as "the greatest juggler on earth." He set out to be the world's best juggler, as Will Rogers had been equally

Will Rogers was President Franklin D. Roosevelt's favorite comedian, invited to the White House five times between 1933 and 1935. No other humorist was in the White House as often during this period. Picture shows President Roosevelt (left) and Rogers.

From a 1920 film, Jes' Call Me John, *with Irene Rich.*

determined to be the world's best roper. And, like Rogers, he became one of the world's funniest comedians.

Ziegfeld took Fields out of vaudeville for the 1915 edition of the *Follies.* Although he served his term from 1915 to 1921, W. C. Fields never obtained top booking as a comedian, always giving way to Fanny Brice, Will Rogers, Eddie Cantor, or Bert Williams.

Unlike Will Rogers, who carried over in his own way the home-spun Yankee humor of an earlier Jonathan, Fields started something of a new school of humor.

But the Fields' brand of humor as well as the comic character he created defied analysis. He had a henpecked aloofness and a terror of small children. His gestures and manner were memor-

W. C. Fields played the part of a ringmaster in the picture Tillie's Punctured Romance. *The lady is Babe London.*

W. C. Fields' famous role as a cardsharp won him laughs throughout his extraordinary career.

able—the way he carried his cane, his tendency to juggle objects, and his apparent disdain for whether or not the audience appreciated or even heard his lines.

Ziegfeld never was able to appreciate Fields' brand of humor and considered him something of a fill-in, to occupy space and time while the girls were changing. On one occasion at the close of one of Fields' sketches, Ziegfeld inquired how long it ran. He was informed that it took approximately one half hour.

"How long does it take the girls to dress for the next scene?" Ziegfeld asked.

"Seven minutes," was the answer.

"Cut the sketch to seven minutes," ordered Ziegfeld.

Fields never fully recovered from this unkind appraisal. Shortly afterward he moved his field of activities to Hollywood. He wrote plays for films, under an odd assortment of pen names such as Otis Criblecoblis or Mahatma Kane Jeeves or simply Charles Vogle, and he acted in them.

On one occasion Fields is reported to have explained to a young lady of his acquaintance that the way he had acquired his red nose was by "bruising it on a cocktail glass in his extreme youth."

On another occasion, Fields sauntered into a hotel carrying his gold-headed cane. His step was jaunty and his hat was slightly dented and frayed. At the desk, Fields rapped in typical fashion and demanded "the bridal suite."

Not recognizing the bland visage, the manager looked at Fields with some degree of fright and informed him that the bridal suite

Eddie Cantor began his career as a singing waiter and learned to blacken his face with burnt cork in an attempt to change his act when breaking into vaudeville. Not a singer, not a dancer, not even a comedian, Cantor was a bundle of nerves in blackface.

was usually reserved for gentlemen with brides.

"That is all right," the comedian answered. "I'll pick up one in town."

Once, Fields found himself in a strange town without companionship. He thereupon started out in search of entertainment. According to the story, he roamed the streets until he saw a lot of vehicles lined up in front of a big house.

"I went up to the door and a butler or somebody stuck a silver plate under my nose. I put an old laundry check and a dime on it and went on in. It was a very enjoyable function. I had a long talk with the Governor's wife."

"What did you talk about, Bill?" he was asked.

"We talked about the mating habits of the Wallaby."

Very different in style from Fields was the young comedian, Eddie Cantor, who came to the *Follies* in 1917. As he recalls it, "When I was with the juggling act, Fanny Brice was already a star. You see, Ziegfeld had the ability to engage the best in each particular field. The best roughhouse comic in the world, without a doubt, was W. C. Fields. The best comedienne, Fanny Brice. The best comedian, Bert Williams, and I guess I had the biggest eyes so Flo hired me."

The Cantor brand of humor was not to captivate the audience by wit or to win laughter by the incongruous. Rather, Cantor tended to overwhelm by his sheer nervous energy, his prancing up and down. Occasionally, he won laughs by playing the role of the weakling in the hands of more powerful forces, such as the osteopath who kneaded his weak limbs like an India rubber doll. Occasionally, however, his humor was verbal and topical.

During the depression of the 1930s, Cantor's special humor dealt with the stock market and the money he and others had lost in speculation.

My throat is cut from ear to ear. I am bleeding profusely in seven other places. There is a knocking in the back of my head, my hands tremble violently, I have sharp shooting pains all over my body, and in addition to all that my general health is none too good.

One of the greatest diagnosticians in America thumped me and probed me all over the premises.

"You are a very sick man!" he said finally. "A very sick man. You are suffering from Montgomery Ward of the liver; General Electric of the stomach; Westinghouse of the brain, and besides you have a severe case of internal combustion."

While the Follies were at their height in New York City, in the faraway village of Hollywood something was happening that would change the entertainment world almost overnight.

Al Shean and Ed Gallagher skyrocketed to fame largely as a result of their Follies *song which included the final tagline: "Positively, Mr. Gallagher?" "Absolutely, Mr. Shean." Such is fame in the entertainment business.*

7

Flickers: From Custard Pie to Cheesecake

At the exact moment that Flo Ziegfeld was capturing the attention of Broadway, across the country another showman of genius was presenting a somewhat similar approach to girls and gags. His name was Mack Sennett and he was what might be called the poor man's Ziegfeld.

Sennett operated in a different medium: the early motion pictures. He slanted his films to a different audience: the masses of people rather than the select few who could afford *Follies* ticket prices. But the two men had much in common. Both took clothes off their women and gained a reputation around the names of their comedians. But each did this in his own special way.

When moving pictures began commercially back in 1905, they were patronizingly referred to as the "flickers" or the "tape," and everybody who knew anything realized that they were but a passing fad, like the horseless carriage.

Moving pictures, however, became an accepted theatrical medium that reflected the need of people for inexpensive entertainment. Motion pictures were revolutionary, beginning a radical change leading to television. Movies changed the working lives of comedians and made entertainment more accessible for mass audiences. People no longer had to wait half the winter for the traveling players to come to town.

The first great comic in the infant film industry was John Bunny, who came from the legitimate theater to the Vitagraph motion picture company when it was located in Brooklyn. Bunny was a huge, happy-looking man with a genius for comic pantomime.

"I didn't want to be a comedian," he said, "but nature was agin' me. How could I expect to play Romeo with a figure like mine? It was many years before I learned to yield gracefully to the fate for which nature had endowed me. I struggled along trying to make managers give me serious parts."

Bunny was a comedian in the tradition of a Charles Dickens comic character. But the infant motion picture industry was destined to be swept into another kind of traditional comedy which featured the physical slapstick of the early buffoon, the throwing of pies, and the downfall of dignity.

Young Mack Sennett was in New York seeking employment in the theater when he heard that professionals might hope to receive as much as $5 a day in the movies. At that time he was playing the hind end of a horse, and consequently he decided that the movies might be a step forward in his career. Sennett was brought to Hollywood from New York by D. W. Griffith, the famous director.

Early in his career, Sennett discovered that he had the knack of recognizing almost instinctively what would make an audience laugh. When a gag failed to make Mack laugh, it usually was not funny to others. From a small-bit actor Sennett shifted to directing comedies for the Keystone Film Company which he founded.

May Irwin, popular comedienne of the legitimate stage, participated in the making of one of the first movies with John C. Rice, entitled The Kiss. *The episode was taken from the climax of their play,* The Widow Jones, *which was playing on Broadway in 1896.*

The early movie machine, the Kinetoscope, which was a sensation in its day.

Sennett was not the only or even the first pioneer in the production of American comedy films. Al Christie produced the first Hollywood film comedy in 1911 and later became the nearest competitor Mack Sennett ever had. Hal Roach, a former movie stunt man and bit player, took to producing comedies in this period too and became one of the most successful in the business.

But Sennett actually had little competition when it came to new techniques for laughter. He revived slapstick, adding new tricks—especially breathtaking speed and pace.

The major Sennett techniques were simple: first, pie throwing; second, the chase, usually featuring the Keystone Cops; and third, bathing beauties.

The making of a Keystone comedy was a free-wheeling operation with a minimum of script or scenario and a maximum of improvising. Directors and players were free to ad lib as they chose as long as additional expense was not involved. It was quite commonplace for several comedians and a cameraman to go off early in the morning in search of incidents for a movie. Whether the scene was a crowded dance hall, a burning building, or a

Technicians of the custard pie soon found that there was nothing funny about a pie which half missed its target. Either the pie "mooned" its object or there was no laugh. Picture shows Mabel Normand, first among the pie throwers, in a pie-tossing scene from A Misplaced Foot, *or* Revenge with a Pie.

runaway horse and wagon, somehow the adventuring comedians managed to turn it into successful slapstick. Such films were made at the rate of one a week.

It was the time of such laughmakers as Roscoe "Fatty" Arbuckle, Hank Mann, Chester Conklin, and Ford Sterling. They were superb comedians by instinct. The humor was physical and

Mack Sennett's fun factory in Los Angeles.

robust. They had no expensive props, no big budgets, no elaborate sets; the scripts were very apt to be written down on someone's cuffs, though Mack Sennett has confessed to writing scripts eight or nine pages long. The scripts were usually torn up halfway through.

The theme of all the Keystone comedies—altogether there were about nine hundred of them—was simplicity itself. They drew from the tradition of farce or broad comedy. Farce included such techniques as slapstick, buffoonery, love regarded as vulgar and physical. This was considered a "low" comedy in contrast to the "high" comedy of wit and manners. The slap stick was originally a real device to focus on the action, one that made a lot of noise but did not hurt the victim-actor. Movement was rapid and rough. Often satirical, the comic action was a ridiculous pretense or an empty show. The jokes were coarse and undignified with gestures and postures made ludicrous by broad exaggeration.

The custard pie was one of the good old reliable laugh-getting techniques which Sennett comedies employed. Credit for throwing the first pie is frequently attributed to Sennett's great comedienne, Mabel Normand. The story goes that a director was vainly trying to make Ben Turpin, the cross-eyed wonder, loosen up and laugh. The cameras were grinding and the director was pleading.

Mabel Normand, who was sitting on the sidelines, observed that several workmen were eating their lunch nearby, and that they had a luscious lemon pie by their side.

A woman of many talents with a devilish sense of humor, she simply walked over, picked up the pie, took aim, and let it fly in the direction of Ben Turpin. It struck the bull's eye or, rather, Ben's eye.

In the meantime, the camera had been cranking, and it recorded the immortal event. Sennett, who had been sitting dourly watching the production, was observed to be laughing uproariously—always a significant sign. When the film was developed, the incident appeared even funnier than it had at the time.

The motion picture audience also appeared to find pie throwing hilarious. From that day on the thrown custard pie ranked high in the arsenal of Sennett comedy tricks. It was said that, " 'Nice people' thought that pie throwing was vulgar and that it was outrageous to laugh at such elemental humor."

There were certain stock situations in the early Sennett films that were always good for a laugh, such as the dramatic ending of the race between Keystone Cops and a train.

If the pie became standard comic technique in the Keystone comedy, so also were the Keystone Cops and the chase which, more likely than not, ended a Keystone comedy. Mack Sennett started every new man as a Keystone Cop to see how he worked out. The cops were a harum-scarum police force who were forever careening madly down roads in zigzagging motorcars with policemen falling off the patrol wagon and climbing aboard again. Keystone Cops took quite a beating in their daily antics and had to know how to fall and how to receive blows without flinching. They were a cross between an acrobat and an imbecile.

"No matter what they did," wrote Richard Watts, Jr., film critic at the time, "from vigorous tumbling to receiving berry pies in the face, the Keystone Cops achieved definite pantomimic effects not like those of stage clowns in their antics but reaching to an entirely new medium."

Audiences looked forward to their antics in every film Sennett produced. Regardless of their connection with the main theme of the film, the capers of the Keystone Cops were a central attraction. Viewers often were so amused that they fell off their seats laughing and rolled in the aisles.

When it came to the attention of Sennett that there always appeared to be space in the press for pretty girls, particularly if their knees were showing, he summoned his staff and said,

67

A platoon of Keystone Cops with Sterling at the phone and Fatty Arbuckle first in line.

as he describes it, "Boys, take a look at this. This is how to get our pictures in the paper. Go hire some girls, any girls, so long as they're pretty, especially around the knees." One step led to another. The next move was to use the beautiful girls collected for publicity purposes in the movies themselves.

"They don't have to act," said Sennett. "Put them in bathing suits and just have them around to be looked at while the comics are making funny." He had learned in burlesque the attraction of a pretty girl, especially if she was not dressed for subzero weather.

Sennett did not present his bathing beauties without sharp opposition, particularly when he designed new bathing suits an inch or two shorter than the prevailing bathing styles. One biographer of Sennett said that his pictures were, in effect, an emancipation proclamation. He simply was giving his audience what they wanted. And he did more in a few years to free the women of America from their horse blanket pagodas than had any other man or woman in centuries of editorializing.

The Mack Sennett comedies continued to be churned out. Most of them were one-reelers, jumpy and jerky, full of unrelated incidents, no plot, little story, and repetitious, but despite all the weaknesses, they were mass entertainment at last.

Among his women stars, Mack Sennett rated Mabel Normand as tops. "To me, she was the greatest comedian that ever lived."

Sennett was not the only one who considered Mabel one of

the most talented. Marie Dressler, herself a star of major magnitude on stage and screen, recalls Mabel:

> I wish I could make you see her as I remember her. Dark, little, vivaciously pretty, as active and as mischievous as a monkey. . . . Always willing to risk life and limb to give the fans a thrill, she used to spend half of her time laid up in a hospital for repairs.
>
> She was an artist's model in New York when Mack Sennett discovered her and gave her a chance in the films. Mabel kept the Keystone lot in gales of laughter, and as a natural wit and tease, she adored plaguing us all. . . .

Even when Mabel Normand gained stardom she would not permit herself to be pampered. She would not allow a substitute or "double" to take her place during hazardous rides, leaps, or falls.

One of the mainstays of the Mack Sennett productions was Ford Sterling, the first Keystone Cop and one of the most popular comedians on the screen. Sterling was rated among the very top three of the comedians, his closest rivals being John Bunny and Max Linder, the French comedian. Sterling had been a clown in the circus and had played all over the country with small stock companies. He was a comedian of a muscular type who fitted in

The lot of a slapstick comedian was not an easy one. Falls from moving vehicles, wild auto rides, races with trains, duckings in ponds, being targets for pies, rocks, and sacks of flour were all in a day's work. But there were redeeming moments too. Mack Swain, a comic reliable, is pictured with a then-unknown Sennett bathing beauty, Gloria Swanson.

69

with the hard chores which made up the slapstick comedy of the day. With him were Fatty Arbuckle in the 300-pound class, and Doc Swain of nearly similar weight who could endure the hardships, the falls, the tumbles, and the pie-throwing, pie-receiving antics that went into the daily lot of the Mack Sennett slapsticks.

Mack Sennett films became favorites from one end of the nation to the other. The stars that Sennett developed had something to do with this, too. The people who passed through the Sennett studios in the early days included Gloria Swanson, Buster Keaton, Carole Lombard, Marie Dressler, Polly Moran, W. C. Fields, Bing Crosby, Ford Sterling, Charlie Murray, Hank Mann, Harry Langdon, Phyllis Haver, Marie Prevost, Mabel Normand, Slim Summerville, Fatty Arbuckle, and a slightly built, timid-looking young man who was to become one of the greatest comedians in the history of the theater, Charlie Chaplin.

Mack Sennett was an innovator. He gave his stars custard pies, but wouldn't let them eat them. He put his girls in bathing suits, but wouldn't let them swim in them.

8

Charlie Chaplin to Mickey Mouse

Mack Sennett had a good eye for figures but a poor memory for names. When it came to recalling that young British comic whom he had seen in New York in the play *Mumming Birds,* the best he could do was recall that the name began with a C. Perhaps it was Chambort or Chadwick.

But whether he remembered the name of the young comic or not, Sennett was shrewd enough to recognize talent when he saw it. Sennett telegraphed his agent and described the man he wanted in detail. There was a delay before he received a telegram.

FELLOW'S NAME CHARLIE CHAPLIN STOP HAS FORTY WEEKS SOLID BOOKING STOP WON'T TAKE CHANCE WITH MOVIES.

Sennett replied, urging his agent to find out what Chaplin was earning on the stage and to offer him three times his salary. Chaplin was then receiving $40 a week. His agent promised him $125 to sign with Keystone. Chaplin agreed, left the troupe that he was playing with, and signed a contract in the late summer of 1913.

Although the deal was done, Sennett had grave misgivings. He had never seen Chaplin offstage and did not know how he would photograph or whether his type of humor would be fitting for the screen.

"When I got the contract," Charlie recalls, "I immediately be-

Comedians helped the sale of Liberty Bonds during World War I. Front row, Marie Dressler and Charlie Chaplin. Standing, left to right, Franklin D. Roosevelt, the Under Secretary of the Navy, Douglas Fairbanks, and Mary Pickford.

gan to attend every picture show where Keystone comedies were being shown. I was terror-struck! I saw Mabel Normand leaping about on the edges of high buildings, jumping from bridges, doing all manner of falls. If they expected that of a woman, what would they expect of me?"

When Charlie presented himself at Sennett's Hollywood studio, the doorman stopped him at the gate, refusing him entrance until he was rescued by Mack Sennett himself.

As Mack Sennett recalls it, it was days and days before Charlie Chaplin put over anything real. "He tried all sorts of makeups— one of them, I remember, was a fat man—but they were all about equally flat. The fact of it was that for some time I felt a little uneasy as to whether my find was a very fortunate one."

Chaplin himself said:

I was a tramp at the beginning and they wanted me to do all the usual slapstick stunts. I had to beg them to let me play the part my way. "If you want somebody to pull all the old gags," I said to Sennett, "why did you hire me? You get a man at $25 to do this sort of stuff!" So at last they gave in to my idea. This I had worked out very carefully; a tramp in a fine hotel—there's a universal situation for you. Hardly a human being hasn't duplicated the feeling of being alone, poor, out of touch with the gay crowd about him, of trying to identify himself somehow with the fine alien throng. So I did the little touches here of imitation—the pulling down of shabby cuffs, the straightening of my hat, all the gestures that give a wider meaning to the characterization.

Mabel Normand recalls, "They didn't really appreciate Charlie in those early days. . . . They were just so used to slapstick that imaginative comedy couldn't penetrate."

The story has often been told of how Chaplin came to adopt the costume for which he became famous. A picture of the Charlie Chaplin character had been in Charlie's mind for a long time. It had come out of his studies of London street types. He then took Mack Swain's mustache, in abbreviated style. He wore Ford Sterling's immense trousers and wore his huge shoes on the wrong feet. Actually, Chaplin did more than borrow Ford's shoes. Both figuratively and literally, Chaplin filled Sterling's shoes, and it was only a short time before Sterling left Sennett's employ to seek work elsewhere. Chaplin had supplanted Sterling as the Number One clown of the Sennett organization.

From the start it was acknowledged that Chaplin would be the

"Comedy must be real and true to life," stated Chaplin. "My comedy is actual life with the slightest twist or exaggeration to bring out what it might be under certain circumstances." When the talkies came, he said that they "come to ruin the world's most ancient art, the art of pantomime."

When Chaplin first came to the Sennett studio he shared the dressing room with the oversized, 300-pound Roscoe "Fatty" Arbuckle, a popular favorite.

sole exception to the custard-pie, Keystone Cop, bathing-beauty routine which was the regular formula for all other Sennett comedians. While Chaplin participated a little in this routine and actually played a Keystone Cop early in his career, he seldom took part in the full formula. It was soon clear that Chaplin had his own type of artistry.

This artistry was to result in a wave of popularity for the Chaplin brand of comedy. Just fourteen months after he had timidly arrived in Hollywood as an employee of Mack Sennett at $125 a week, Chaplin left the Sennett studio to join the Essanay film-making company for $1,250 a week. The following year, 1916, Chaplin was making $10,000 a week and a bonus of $150,000 when he signed with the Mutual Film Corporation. And the year after that, Chaplin was earning no less than $1,075,000 for eight two-reel pictures with the First National Exhibitors Circuit.

In an interview in this early period, Chaplin remarked that it only took about two weeks' work at the Keystone plant to make him very enthusiastic about pictures, especially farces.

> I study the screen closely now, and I am firmly convinced that everyone in the industry should do likewise. There are many things that we can learn from it, even though we think we have perfected ourselves in our own line of the great industry.

74

I endeavor to put nothing in my farces which is not a burlesque on something in real life. No matter how senseless a thing may seem on the screen, I think that if it is studied carefully it can be traced back to life, and is probably an everyday occurrence which the would-be critic of the farce had thought to be a bit funny.

A typical Chaplin film gem is *Shoulder Arms*. Charlie is a "doughboy" during World War I. Here's how Theodore Huff, Chaplin biographer, describes it:

In the first scene Charlie is a member of the "Awkward Squad" in a training camp. We see him at drill and the sergeant ordering, "Put those feet in!" Trying to obey the drill commands, Charlie tangles himself up as the rest of the squad march off. He catches up with the others, to go into a sequence of in-turning and out-turning of his toes accompanied by barked commands. At dismissal Charlie hops to his tent to fall exhausted on his cot (fade out).

"Over there." Charlie staggers in under knapsacks, rifle, blankets, household utensils, etc. Tapping an officer on the shoulder for directions, he walks forward (moving camera) to a sign labeled: *Broadway and Rotten Row*. The new recruit is put through an inspection by a sergeant who gets his fingers caught in provident Charlie's rat trap. With his billowing equipment he gets stuck in the dugout door and is helped through, finally, by a boot from the sergeant. His first act, when he reaches his quarters is to hang up a nutmeg grater to scratch his back on, the "cooties" having already "occupied" him.

The scene shifts to the enemy trenches where a pint-size, goose-stepping German officer carries on an inspection, consisting mainly of kicks. Back in Charlie's trench, he and the sergeant enjoy a "quiet lunch" during the shelling. Charlie is told to make himself at home as his helmet bounces around with the detonations.

Alongside of giants Arbuckle and Mack Swain, Chaplin appeared almost insignificant.

Later Charlie is standing guard in pouring rain, dreaming of home. In a split screen effect we see, on the left, a New York street scene dissolving to a bartender serving drinks. As Charlie smiles, the vision fades back to the muddy trench. The guard is changed, and the miserable soldier marches to his bed and lies down—all in rhythm.

A postman brings "news from home." Charlie rushes forward, only to hear everybody's name called but his own. Sitting on his bunk, he leans disconsolately on his elbow. As Sid and another soldier open food packages, Charlie, refusing snacks offered by his buddies, nibbles the cheese in his trap. Sauntering outside, moodily he looks over the shoulder of a man reading a letter and reacts vicariously as if it were his own, smiling when the other man smiles, or registering concern. He leans forward for a closer look, smiles again—until the soldier glares and moves away.

The mailman returns. "This must be yours." Charlie frantically opens his package—to extract a dog biscuit and Limberger cheese. Protecting himself with a gas mask he tosses the cheese like a grenade across No Man's Land into the enemy trenches. It lands on the face of the little German officer just as he is toasting their early arrival in Paris.

"Bedtime" finds the little dugout half filled with water. Only the sergeant's head and his feet, with a frog perched on one of them, shows above the water. Charlie lifts his pillow out of the water, to fluff it before he lies down, then pulls the sopping blanket over him. The sergeant's snoring is so effective that when Charlie scoops water over to his open mouth, a geyser results. Splashing back at him, the sergeant orders him to "Stop rocking the boat!" A lighted candle comes floating by and Charlie blows it, like a little sailboat, toward Sid's protruding toes, and plays innocent when the hot-footed man awakes. Charlie hunts a more comfortable spot at the other end of the bunk only to have his head submerge. With the help of a phonograph horn as a breathing tube, he settles down to a submarine snooze.

As zero hour approaches next morning Charlie finds that his identification tag is number 13. Pulling a mirror out of his pocket he primps as a means of bracing his courage. Ordered "over the top," Charlie rushes heroically up the ladder which hurtles back into the mud. "13 is not so unlucky."

He is next seen herding a line of captured Germans, among them the little officer, whom Charlie takes on his lap for a spanking. This

Chaplin and Ford Sterling were rivals in real life as well as on the screen, as in top photo, left. Right, top, Chaplin in The Immigrant. Lower left, Chaplin and Jackie Coogan in The Kid. Lower right, Chaplin in Shoulder Arms.

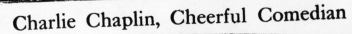

Charlie Chaplin, Cheerful Comedian

Though this title tells little,
of a doubt, is the funniest man
asserted, without coming far fro
There remains little to be s

FOUR MORE DAYS LEFT FOR CHAPLIN CONTEST

By this time all of you who have applied must have your
back copies of last week's Evening Journal for the Charlie
Chaplin contest. You have until Saturday midnight to send
them in—four more days.

You can thank the extraordinary
success of the contest for your

erly assembled, on a blank sheet
of paper so that they form a com-

Isn't Cha

THE curiously assorted bill at th

New Stunt---Imitating a Popular Film Player

STAGE ENTRANCE

CHAPLIN CONTEST TO·NIGHT

More Than Thirty Picture Houses Have Amateur Chaplin Nights. Here Are Some of the Amateurs.

The Real Charlie Chaplin
The Personal Side of the Famous Comedian as His Associates Know It

Why Is Charlie Chaplin?

*The Chaplin craze swept the nation. Clippings give a brief indication
of the variety of newspaper notices. Chaplin was seldom satisfied with
his own performances. "It's a desperate business being a clown," he
once said.*

earns him the admiration of a huge German soldier, who shakes his
head. Asked how he captured them, Charlie makes the now classic
reply, "I surrounded them."

With the tremendous interest in Chaplin films came a wave of
Chaplinism which spread to every corner of the nation as well as
the entire world. Theaters held amateur contests for Chaplin imitations. Many a comedian got by solely on his ability to imitate
Chaplin. There was scarcely a child in the United States at the
time who hadn't at some point taken a cane, painted a false mus-

tache on himself, and walked across the room imitating Chaplin.

As Bob Hope recalls, "Charlie Chaplin imitations had made me show-business conscious. I'd put on my Chaplin makeup and walk duck-legged down to the corner past the firehouse. I twirled a rattan cane and wore flapping, oversized battered shoes. Amateur Charlie Chaplin contests had broken out in the country's theaters like a rash. I was so good at it that I was persuaded to enter a contest at Luna Park. To make sure I won, my brothers rounded up all the neighborhood kids to vote for me."

The influence of Charlie Chaplin in the world of comedy can hardly be exaggerated. The new medium of motion pictures was thirsting for popular heroes, sufficiently sensitive to appeal to the people's hearts and native sense of humor which is always so close to the tragic. Chaplin's talents and sympathies lent themselves admirably to satisfy this need. But he was by no means the only major figure in the laugh-making business of the early silent films.

Motion pictures for the first time gave entertainers an audience of millions. Jack Bunny, Mack Sennett, and Charlie Chaplin were among the pioneers in movie laugh making, but they were challenged for top laurels by an ever-increasing number of funnymen. Among the first of these challengers was Harold Lloyd, whose box-office accomplishments even surpassed Chaplin in certain peak years. Lloyd opened the way for a parade of popular film comedians whose names helped make Hollywood a golden mecca for film folks.

When Lloyd first came to Hollywood, he found himself rejected. Even the shrewd Mack Sennett bounced him from his studio as a person without ability. Hal Roach, by now a producer

Harold Lloyd on the bottom in a scene from The Freshman.

Lloyd was one of the first movie comedians to use trick photography in a professional way. He would dangle by his heels, seemingly far above city streets, walk narrow girders, escape plunging to his destruction by an eyelash. Actually, he was only a few feet from solid ground when such a picture as the one at right was taken.

of successful comedy films, showed keener judgment and teamed up with Lloyd to make a series of early comic shorts.

At first Lloyd found it difficult to resist the Chaplin influence, but in time he invented a comic character which allowed him to be funny in his own right.

The character he devised was "quiet, normal, boyish, clean, sympathetic," as Lloyd described him. The humor derived from the difference between the character and the scrapes he fell into. Lloyd had no need of putty noses or funny clothes. His only prop was a pair of horn-rimmed glasses which added to his air of innocence, therefore accentuating the discrepancy between the character and the situations he found himself in. As Lloyd himself describes it:

> There is more magic in a pair of horn-rimmed glasses than the opticians dream of, nor did I guess the half of it when I put them on in 1917.
>
> With them, I am Harold Lloyd; without them, a private citizen. I can stroll unrecognized down any street in the land at any time without the glasses, a boon granted to no other picture star and one which some of them would pay well for. At a cost of seventy-five cents they provide a trademark recognized instantly wherever pictures are shown. They make low-comedy clothes unnecessary, per-

mit enough romantic appeal to catch the feminine eye, usually averted from comedies, and they hold me down to no particular type or range of story.

Lloyd Hamilton was a favorite with his pancake hat and duck-like walk. Some believe that he influenced Jackie Gleason in his style of walking.

Harry Langdon was popular despite the fact that he usually seemed on the verge of tears. With his baby face and childlike innocence, he was a forerunner of the Gobel type of humor of more recent years.

Another comedian who was a formidable rival for the "funniest" was Buster Keaton, the "great stone face" of the silent era.

Keaton entered the entertainment business at the age of three when he accompanied his mother and father on the stage as one of "The Three Keatons." He was thrown about on the stage and into the orchestra, sometimes landing on his back, but always getting a laugh for his pratfalls. When the early movies were in the market for comedy types, Keaton applied and became one of Mack Sennett's many finds.

You might not guess the identity of any of the three below unless you were a confirmed movie goer of several decades ago. Left to right: Chester Conklin, Leo, the walking lion, and W. C. Fields in Tillie's Punctured Romance.

The young man on the right may look familiar. Starting from the left: Buster Keaton, Polly Moran, and, you've guessed it, Jimmy Durante in the silent movie, Her Cardboard Lover. *Behind his great stone face, Keaton was a keen student of comedy. "The best way to get a laugh," he said, "is to create a genuine thrill and then relieve the tension with comedy."*

Keaton, like Harold Lloyd, had to establish some character type. This turned out to be a character with a blank, expressionless face—as devoid of human emotion as a dishpan. Some people insist that Keaton at his prime in the 1920s was second to none in comedy. His flat top hat and his blank visage applied to hilarious comedy situations was a sure laughmaker. Roughhouse was Keaton's stock in trade, and whether he was thrust head first into a cannon or tossed from a burning building, he kept his face as composed as if he were sipping cocktails in a lounge. It was only the arrival of talking pictures that cut short Keaton's vast popularity. After a lapse of many years, he reappeared in films for theater and television.

Another great comedienne of the period and an admirer of Chaplin was Marie Dressler. She was one of the most beloved women on the stage and, in her later life, in the movies. She started

Marie Dressler, a friend of seven presidents, favorite of the legitimate stage of the 1880s, became a silent motion picture star late in her career. Not content with that, she teamed up with Wallace Beery to make a tremendous success of the talkie, Min and Bill. *Marie became* Tugboat Annie *to a new generation.*

her career in legitimate theater, where she became an outstanding comedienne. She played with Eddie Foy, Weber and Fields, and other notables. She moved into vaudeville circles and achieved a national reputation there. While in vaudeville, she was observed by that ever-ready scout of comedy, Mack Sennett, who invited her to come to Hollywood.

Though a woman past her youth, Marie went to Hollywood and participated in the making of one of the first full-length comedy pictures, *Tillie's Punctured Romance*, with Charlie Chaplin and Mabel Normand.

Marie Dressler was a favorite with the World War I G.I.s. One of the first detachments to land in France named a street and a cow after her. "The boys had a lot of fun with my bovine namesake," said Marie Dressler. "She gave so much rich sweet milk and cream that one company was always stealing her from another. Company A would march off one morning secure in the possession of Dressler, only to find when they returned to their billets that she was contentedly munching fodder in Company B's stable.

Wallace Beery and Raymond Hatton played together in silent films. Here the pair move a piano. As usual, Hatton ended up carrying the entire load with Beery supervising. In the early comedy films, Beery impersonated a woman.

Stan Laurel and Oliver Hardy were perhaps the most popular box-office attraction of their time.

"One bright day, I woke up to find headlines screaming, 'Marie Dressler killed in line of duty.' The text beneath explained that it was the cow, not the actress, who had been felled by the enemy. Nevertheless, I had a hard time convincing people that the report of my death had been greatly exaggerated."

Marie Dressler remained in Hollywood when the talking pictures arrived. Because of early stage experience, she became one of the outstanding stars of the early talking pictures.

Zazu Pitts had a meek and resigned humor all her own.

Will Rogers seldom agreed to use makeup in his films. Rare picture shows him applying makeup to his weather-beaten face.

"I was born homely," she used to say, "and for fifty years it has been my lot to make a living on the stage where the first requisite for a woman's success is supposed to be a face that's easy on the eyes. I was born serious and I have earned my bread by making other people laugh . . . when everything else fails I get my voice down to the audience and make a face."

The new motion picture industry had not succeeded in displacing the legitimate theater. Although more people laughed at a mouse in a week than laughed at a Broadway show in many months, still the "legit" carried on.

Mickey Mouse, a Walt Disney creation, has been, without doubt, the most widely admired rodent in all history. While he did not succeed Chaplin as a center of attention, he did win a vast audience from people of all ages. Unlike Chaplin, Lloyd, and other comedians, Mickey never seems to grow old.

9

The "Legit" Carries On

It was hard to tell from the bright lights glowing along Broadway in the 1920s that the legitimate theater and vaudeville were about to suffer a crushing blow.

If you looked closely, however, you could read signs that all was not well. For instance, clauses were placed in many contracts forbidding motion picture work. Nevertheless, public attendance at the movies mounted because of the low admission price.

But the world of flesh-and-blood entertainment seemed to be booming, and no voice boomed louder than that of Al Jolson. His one brief encounter with the silent films had soured him temporarily on ever again leaving the legitimate theater.

Al Jolson got his start in the early 1900s as a burnt-cork singer in Lou Dockstadter's minstrel.

On the legitimate stage, Jolson was a human tornado and he took Broadway by storm. "He flings into a comic song or three-minute impersonation so much energy, violence, so much of the totality of one human being," wrote a critic of the time, "that you feel it would suffice for a hundred others."

Jolson's "you ain't heard nothin' yet" was not just a comic expression. It represented an actual attitude of Jolson's toward his audience because the man could keep singing, dancing, and joking for as long as there were laughs available from the audience.

Al Jolson painfully worked his way to the top of the ladder, emerging as the king of show business. One critic acknowledged sheepishly, "I must admit that when Jolson gets on stage, I forget

"Al Jolson," wrote Joe Laurie, Jr., "was the greatest of all American entertainers." Jolson proudly referred to himself as a comedian.

all about the play's deficiencies . . . there is only one Jolson and he is a natural force as great as the Mississippi."

The secret of Jolson's attraction was in the inexhaustible supply of energy that he poured into every lyric and every movement, and his incomparable faculty for captivating the hearts of his audience. He went a long way toward making people actually believe the words, no matter how ridiculous, of the song he was singing.

There is a story that goes that when Jolson's talents were employed by a phonograph company to make gramophone records in the early days, Jolson found it exceedingly difficult to sit still and direct his songs right into the big horn. He could only stay still for a moment or two and then he would be up prancing about.

In desperation, the phonograph company executives hired two employees to hold him down. They tried their best but Jolson kept squirming out of their grasp. Finally, as a gag, a straitjacket was procured and the protesting Jolson was placed in it and then ordered to do his recording.

"I'm the only man in the world who recorded in a straitjacket," he later told his friends.

Another great comic was Bobby Clark, who started his long career at laugh making in a minstrel show in the early 1900s. He served as a clown in the circus, in vaudeville, and then in burlesque. Clark joined with Paul McCullough, and the team of Clark and McCullough became one of the most successful comedy teams in legitimate show business.

Clark was strictly a prop man and always depended on physical antics and his famous leer to provide the laughs. His cigar, his cane, and his painted-on glasses were trademarks of his humor.

The story is that as a clown in the early days, he wore shell-rimmed glasses. One day he mislaid them and frantically hit upon the idea of painting on the glasses in their place. He has worn them ever since.

"I guess I'll die with them on," Clark says. "Managers won't have me otherwise."

Ed Wynn, who wore silly hats, crazy costumes, and huge shoes, pretended to lisp in a high-pitched voice and giggled at the slightest provocation.

He was one of the first major comedians to eliminate slapstick from his repertoire. His act was more that of sidewalk conversa-

*There was something about Jolson which made him top man in what-
ever field of entertainment he entered. He didn't have a great voice,
but he was a great singer. He didn't have a clever patter of jokes, but
he made people laugh. Some say it was his energy; others, his personality; but most everyone agreed he was King of Entertainers.*

tion. His sure laugh getters were his many inventions, such as the
corn-on-the-cob typewriter carriage which would ring a bell when
the eater reached the end of a line; or the use of a pair of mechan-
ical windshield wipers for eyeglasses when eating grapefruit.
Wynn used many labor-saving devices on the stage. Dragging a
toy wagon before the footlights, he took from it a safety device
for noiseless soups, or a coffee cup with a hole in the bottom (to
save the labor of pouring the coffee into the saucer).

Wynn was one of the first recognized masters of ceremonies,
having started in 1913 on the opening bill of the Palace Theatre,
the pinnacle in American vaudeville. When something went
wrong with the signs announcing the sequence of acts, Wynn,
with an act on the bill also, announced the acts in person. Soon
jokes were added and Wynn became a part of each act on the
bill. The same technique, which was later proposed by Wynn to
Ziegfeld when he played in the *Follies*, became a standard one
for *Follies'* comedians after that.

Wynn, a shrewd judge of his fellow comedians, coaxed W. C.
Fields into speaking lines during his juggling act when Fields
was a silent *Follies* comedy juggler. It was also Wynn who convinced Will Rogers to do more than spin ropes and to add yarns

to his repertoire. "Rogers was the funniest man I ever heard in private," Wynn recalls, "but he didn't dare say anything when on the stage. He took the plunge and became one of the funniest comedians Ziegfeld ever had."

Later in life it was Ed Wynn who started the vogue of joshing the radio commercials. "I'll stick to my horse, Graham," he would lisp to Graham McNamee, the announcer, when he was proclaiming a gasoline commercial.

The unique characteristic of Ed Wynn has been his amazing ability to adapt his genuine comic spirit to changing conditions. His career has encompassed many personalities: the Rah, Rah, Rah Boy; the Boy with the Funny Hat; the King's Jester; the Perfect Fool; the Fire Chief. A generation of radio listeners can recall the comic Ed Wynn letter-answering service as part of the Fire Chief program.

A typical laugh getter in Ed Wynn's letter-answering department was this:

Dear Chief:
I am a woman of forty-five years of age. I weigh 187 pounds and have just rented an apartment which is in a court. There are no window shades in the bathroom and I am afraid of taking a bath because my neighbors can see in. My landlord won't buy shades. What shall I do?
Out of Shape

Ed Wynn's answer would go something like this:

Dear Out of Shape:
If you are really forty-five years of age and if you really weigh 187 pounds, your landlord doesn't have to buy you window shades. You take a bath and your neighbors will buy the shades.
Fire Chief

Joe Cook was a fast-talking comedian who left his audience breathless and exhausted. As a monologist, he had few superiors unless it was "Doc" Rockwell, the original "quack, quack, quack" man of vaudeville and legitimate theater. Using a skull or banana stalk to illustrate his "scientific" lectures, Rockwell would present a devastating stream of patter.

George Moran and Charlie Mack, the "Two Black Crows," were

Ed Wynn, "The Perfect Fool."

a comedy team with a line that went something like this:

MORAN: I hear your folks are getting rid of all your horses.

MACK: Only the white horses, they eat too much.

MORAN: You mean to say the white horses eat more than the others?

MACK: Yes, the white horses eat twice as much as the black horses.

MORAN: How do you explain that?

MACK: There's twice as many of them. We have four white horses and two black horses. So we're getting rid of the white horses and we're going to get black ones.

Joe E. Brown was another old trouper with years on the legitimate stage, a comedian of the old clown type, a mugger by trade. His unusually large mouth and comical expression won him laughs when he deserved them for no other reason. "At some time or other, every comedian wants to be a tragedian and every tragedian wants to be a comedian," Brown commented. "But comedy has always been my forte. . . . I always considered the physical defects I was born with were tragedy enough." His style is evoked by the following:

Did you ever make a telephone call from one of those streamlined drugstore phone booths—the kind which are almost form-fitting? asks Brown.

I got into one once that was so suffocatingly small that I could barely close the door. And I had to close the door before the light would go on.

Then I found that I couldn't get the phone book far enough from my eyes to read it. In order to get some distance I pushed the door open—while still holding the book open in both hands—and the light went out.

91

Joe Jackson has been described as "the greatest comedy act on or off a bicycle." A pantomimist of rare talent, Jackson won a vast following especially in vaudeville, repeating his same tramp bike-riding act year in and year out. When he died, his son, Joe Jackson, Jr., capably followed in his father's bicycle tracks. Modern television comedians envy this ability to repeat a single comedy act for two generations.

I tried to carry the book outside the booth to look at it, but it was chained to the telephone.

The theater of the early part of the twentieth century featured many talented comedians, some of whom had had their start in burlesque, the minstrel show, and the early *Ziegfeld Follies*. Both vaudeville and the legitimate theater featured Fanny Brice, Eddie Cantor, Bobby Clark, George M. Cohan, Marie Dressler, W. C. Fields, Frank Tinney, Eddie Foy, DeWolf Hopper, May Irwin, Al Jolson, Bert Lahr, Victor Moore, Fred Stone, Weber and Fields, Ed Wynn, Nat Wills, and many more during this period.

The legitimate theater was to provide a range of comedy from *Abie's Irish Rose,* which played over 2,300 consecutive performances in New York, to *Hellzapoppin',* which held sway at the Winter Garden for a seemingly endless period of time. The effervescent energy of Al Jolson and the perfect foolishness of Ed Wynn provided flesh-and-blood mirth for legitimate theaters.

But even the genius of such comedians was not able in any way to hide the fact that the legitimate theater had received a sledgehammer blow from the youthful movies. Evidence of this was in the trek of the stars to Hollywood and the fact that vaudeville, born in 1883, finally withered and died in 1932. Some say that it actually never died but merely changed its form.

There were some people during this early period who refused to recognize the threat of the motion pictures.

Nevertheless, if the silent films seriously threatened the legitimate theater, the coming of talkies sounded the death knell of vaudeville, helped bury burlesque, and created such serious problems for the legitimate theater that it has not to this day been able to solve them fully.

10

For Laughing Out Loud

It's been well known for a long time that talking can get you into a lot of trouble. Any comedian can tell you that. But how much trouble?

Nobody would have guessed.

Not only did talking movies help bury vaudeville, minstrels, burlesque, the circus, and much of nightclubbing, they also threw scores of super movie stars out of work. Ever since old Dr. Lee DeForest produced a film in 1923 that showed a man dropping a load of empty pie trays *and* reproduced the noise, sound motion pictures have been on the horizon. Of course, nobody seriously believed that talking movies would ever challenge the silent films.

But one day the nation woke up to discover that talking pictures were an improvement on silent films. The American public welcomed them with open ears.

Don Juan, featuring John Barrymore, was one of the earliest successful talking pictures.

Al Jolson, whose early experiences with silent movies had soured him with the industry, finally had agreed to star in the screen production of *The Jazz Singer*, a highly successful theatrical show on Broadway starring Georgie Jessel, a talented comedian and entertainer.

The Jazz Singer on the screen was not all talkie. As a matter of fact, all the audience could hear was Jolson singing one song and muttering his famous, "You ain't heard nothin' yet." But that was enough. The semi-talkie was an immense success. More people

saw and heard Jolson in a week than had ever heard of him previously.

Some vaudeville acts were leery of movie offers since they suspected—and this proved to be true in the long run—that this was one of the best ways to demolish a perfectly good act. As a result, many of the vaudeville headliners who went West actually did so only after hurriedly creating a brand-new show for Hollywood use. They kept the old shows for the reliable vaudeville billings which were still the steady bread and butter.

Among the early talking pictures was *Coconuts,* featuring four rollicking, hare-brained, disreputable-appearing advocates of slapstick and roughhouse who called themselves the Four Marx Brothers.

(The Marx Brothers were actually five in number. They gradually whittled down to four and finally emerged as three.)

Coconuts was a hilarious success. The Marx Brothers, who could not have been in silent films and still been true to their particular type of comedy, proved tremendous on the talking screen. This picture started the brothers on a long career of frantic comedy which did much to alter the course of fun-making in the United States. Later Groucho was the star of a popular TV show, "You Bet Your Life."

A verbal description of the Marx Brothers' type of comedy presents difficulties. Perhaps the nearest approach would be to imagine, if you can, painting a mustache on the upper lip of a fierce and mature bull, placing a lit cigar between his lips, teaching him to play the harp and the piano, and having him speak English with an Italian accent. Then turn him loose in a china shop. This is the Marx Brothers.

The brothers came to the talkies via Broadway where they had succeeded in destroying scenery, musical instruments, and entire orchestras in musical comedies to the overwhelming approval of their enthusiastic audiences. They were Harpo, Groucho, Chico, Zeppo, and Gummo.

Here is a sample of typical Marx Brothers' humor.

GROUCHO: Do you know what a blueprint is?
CHICO: Sure, oysters.
GROUCHO: We're going to have an auction.
CHICO: I came over here on the Atlantic Auction.

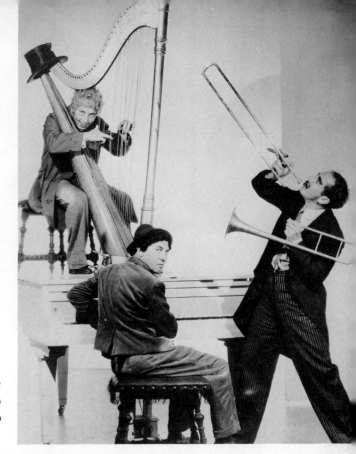

The three Marx Brothers: Harpo at the harp; Chico at the piano; and Groucho at the horn.

GROUCHO: We have a quota. Do you know what a quota is?
CHICO:　　Sure, I got a quota (he takes a coin out of his pocket).

Groucho was always master of the zany monologue. Here he is as auctioneer at a sale of land:

Now, folks, we'll take Lot Number 25. Right over there where you're standing. Say, would you mind taking your feet off that lot? You're getting it dirty. Now here's a lot. Oh, I know it doesn't look very big on top, but it goes down as far as you want to go. Now, then, what am I offered for Lot Number 25? What am I offered for Lot Number 25 and a set of O. Henry? What am I offered for O. Henry? Does anybody want to buy a set of dishes? I'll wrestle anybody in the crowd for five bucks.

After a brief interruption, Groucho continues:

Eight hundred residences will be built right here. They are as good as up. Better. You can have any kind of house you want. You can even get stucco. Oh, how you can get stucco. Now is the time to buy while the new boom is on. Remember a new boom sweeps

The Marx Brothers produced a series of motion pictures, each one zanier than the other, including: Coconuts, A Day at the Races, A Night at the Opera, Room Service.

clean. And don't forget the guarantee. If these lots don't double themselves in a year, I don't know what you can do about it.

Talkies were a perfect medium for most comedians. One such was Red Skelton, whose type of wild physical comedy established him as one of the leading of the nation's comedians. Like Groucho, Skelton was a master at the ad lib or spontaneous remark. As a friend once said:

Directing Red Skelton is like packing a trunk. You always have twice as much stuff as you have room for. You start with a carefully worked out schedule, a perfectly timed script. On the very next scene, Red comes up with an idea for a bit of business or a line of funny dialogue.

"But we haven't room for it, Red," I protest.

"I won't take but a minute," Skelton says.

It's too good to ignore. We include it in the scene. Then comes the question: What will we drop out to make room for it? "Oh, well," I think, "we'll make that up by dropping something out later."

That never works. The next scene finds Red once more popping up with a new and fancy bit that we add. He is a veritable fountain of comedy lines and business. One gag line reminds him of another and that one of still one more.

Among the new comedians whom the talking films brought forward was a thin, wiry, red-haired young man by the name of Danny Kaye, a product of New York nightclubs. His versatility included singing, dancing, and comic pantomime comparable to the greatest comedians. His entry into the moving pictures was sensational, with *Up in Arms* reaching worldwide success. Danny has shown great interest in the world as his audience and he has been called "The Uncrowned King of English Entertainment."

Much of Danny's free time has been devoted to the United Nations International Children's Emergency Fund. He took a trip around the world for UNICEF equipped with a cameraman. The result was a documentary called *Assignment Children,* distributed nationally as a public service by Paramount Pictures with all proceeds going to UNICEF.

Another innovator in talking pictures was Robert Benchley, former theater critic and vaudeville comedian. Benchley's type of humor was at the opposite pole from that of the Marx Brothers. Being completely without props of any kind—unless a starched white shirt and a sheaf of papers are props—his costume was a street suit, his characterization presumably that of himself: a meek, self-conscious, average man-about-town. His early shorts

Jimmy, the well-dressed man. Jimmy Durante was one of the many Broadway entertainers who found Hollywood's talking films a perfect medium for his talents.

Danny Kaye, dancer, singer, master of mimicry, and a comedian of ability.

such as his famous *The Treasurer's Report* became classics in the talking film industry:

> I shall take but a very few moments of your time this evening, for I realize that you would much rather be listening to this interesting entertainment than to a dry financial statement . . . but I *am* reminded of a story—which you have probably all of you heard.
>
> It seems that there were these two Irishmen walking down the street when they came to a—oh, I should have said in the first place that the parrot which was hanging out in *front* of the store—or rather belonging to one of these fellows—the *first* Irishman, that is—was—well, *anyway*, this parrot—
>
> Now in connection with reading this report, there are one or two points which Dr. Murnie wanted brought up in connection with it, and he has asked me to bring them up in connec—to bring them up.

In the first place, there is the question of the work which we are trying to do up there at our little place at Silver Lake, a work which we feel not only fills a very definite need in the community but also fills a very definite need—er—in the community. I don't think that many members of the Society realize just how big the work is that we are trying to do up there. For instance, I don't think that it is generally known that most of our boys are between the age of fourteen. We feel that, by taking the boy at this age, we can get closer to his real nature—for a boy *has* a very real nature, you may be sure —and bring him into closer touch not only with the school, the parents, and with each other, but also with the town in which they live, the country to whose flag they pay allegiance, and to the—ah—town in which they live.

Now the fourth point which Dr. Murnie wanted brought up was that in connection with the installation of the new furnace last Fall. There seems to have been considerable talk going around about this not having been done quite as economically as it might-have-been-done, when, as a matter of fact, the whole thing *was* done just as economically as possible—in fact, even *more* so. I have here a report of the Furnace Committee, showing just how the whole thing was handled from start to finish.

. . . Now, these figures bring us down only to October. In October my sister was married, and the house was all torn up, and in the general confusion we lost track of the figures for May and August.

Judy Holliday's funny style went from Broadway to Hollywood with great success.

Abbott and Costello went from vaudeville to films still seen on television.

Joe E. Brown was able to translate humor from stage to film.

All those wishing the *approximate* figures for May and August, however, may obtain them from me in the vestry after the dinner, where I will be with pledge cards for those of you who wish to subscribe over and above your annual dues, and I hope that each and every one of you here tonight will look deep into his heart and (archly) into his pocketbook, and see if he can not find it there to help us to put this thing over with a bang (accompanied by a wholly ineffectual gesture representing a bang) and to help and make this just the biggest and best year the Armenians have ever had . . . I thank you.

Once on their way, the talking motion pictures devoured everything within sight. Their charm was irresistible, their influence tremendous. Within three years after the first talking motion picture, twenty thousand out of twenty-two thousand motion picture theaters in the country had rewired for sound. Comedians such

George Moran and Charlie Mack (Two Black Crows), seen in early films, originated on the Broadway stage.

Red Skelton carried on the traditional physical clown comedy which has been a steady laugh provoker since memory began. Here he is shown exhibiting one of his many talents in a talkie, Public Pigeon No. 1.

Among the comedians who went into talkies was a song-and-dance man named Bob Hope. Soon the nation was laughing at Hope's jokes and it has been laughing ever since.

as W. C. Fields, Burns and Allen, Fanny Brice, Will Rogers, Eddie Cantor, and Al Jolson became stars of the talking films.

Whereas their audiences previously were somewhat limited, they now reached millions from one end of the country to the other, wherever a motion picture theater was located. Not only were the faces of the stars projected nationally and internationally as in the days of the silent films, but their voices, their intonations, their personalities, the very breath they drew, the very sighs they uttered became part of the folklore of the country.

Who would have guessed that the mighty talking motion picture—that had so greedily rushed to destroy great sections of the legitimate theatrical entertainment world—was itself to be half-devoured by still a newer entertainment medium?

The Three Stooges hold some sort of record for longevity. Moe Howard, Larry Fine, and Shemp Howard began the two-reel comedy series in 1933. The team continued uninterruptedly. When one of the trio, Shemp Howard, died in 1957, he was replaced by Joe Besser. The Three Stooges issued over two hundred short comedies.

II

Laughmakers: By Night and By Day

Nightclubs provided a setting in which comedians could perform. This was particularly important since the movies had killed burlesque and vaudeville. Moreover, comedians helped develop nightclubs, which obtained their start in the days of Prohibition following World War I. It was a federal crime to buy an alcoholic drink and special clubs or "speakeasies" were established mainly to sell liquor underground. Those were hectic days and the flaunting of the Prohibition Law tended to encourage the establishment of the nightclub.

The comedian has played an important part in the nightclub in all of its stages of development.

During Prohibition days, one of the most famous of all nightclub comedians to come to the fore was Jimmy Durante. Texas Guinan, Van and Schenck, Harry Richman, and others built their following in clubs. Jimmy always felt that there was a difference in technique between working in the intimate space of a nightclub and the vastly greater one of the theater.

It was during his nightclub days that Jimmy received the name of "Schnozzola." As he describes it, "Jack Duffy of the vaudeville team of Bernard and Duffy christened me . . . came into the Alamo one night and I asked him to do a number. 'Sure, Schnozzola,' he said, 'What will it be?' Before that I had always been 'Ragtime Jimmy,' now I'll never be anything but Schnozzola."

Jimmy had been merely a nightclub piano player up to the time he met Lou Clayton and Eddie Jackson, both dancers and able nightclub entertainers. The team of Clayton, Jackson, and Durante was to become one of the most successful comedy teams in the history of American entertainment. Occasionally Jimmy would leave the piano to engage in a little singing. Up to that time he had never cracked a joke. As he put it, "Once in a while I would sing a song through one of dem megraphones. But I didn't even do much singin'. I never had much of a verce."

Encouraged by friends, in particular, Sime Silverman, editor of *Variety,* the trio opened up their own nightclub. They decided to call the enterprise the Club Durante, but when the sign was installed, Jimmy noticed that it read "Club Durant." Jimmy protested that an "e" was missing. But the person in charge said that an additional "e" would cost an additional $100. Since money was short, the partners decided to let the sign stand as it was; one of the most famous of all nightclub spots went down in history with a misspelled name.

It was not long before the Club Durant became the rage of New York with the team of Clayton, Jackson, and Durante engaging in the beginnings of their type of roughhouse, wildman comedy which became the sensation of the nightclub after-dark crowd. Upon visiting the Club Durant, George M. Cohan murmured, "Don't those guys ever sit down?"

While the team of Clayton, Jackson, and Durante was a talented one, it became apparent that Jimmy provided the touch of lovable genius which was creating a national entertainment sensation. Durante's nose was on its way—as Gene Fowler put it—to "becoming the most widely known promontory this side of Gibraltar."

The fact is that Jimmy Durante, through his nightclub entertainment, brought something new to the American comedy scene. He, together with Clayton and Jackson, introduced a form of whirlwind comedy, physical in its major aspects with its hat-throwing, piano-breaking, mad-clown antics. But there was something more to it than rough-and-tumble shenanigans which characterized the Clayton, Jackson, and Durante bill of fare. The spark which ignited the team was Jimmy himself and his spontaneous type of humor which seemed to flow from him as naturally as mutterings from a W. C. Fields or a Mammy song from an Al Jolson.

When Jimmy left nightclubbing he had some doubt that he

Yes, that's Jimmy Durante at the "pianner." He is with a group of youthful nightclub entertainers in the early days of his career. "He would be a great comic even with a snub nose," one critic commented.

Joe E. Lewis, talented nightclub comedian, used to be confused with the fighter, Joe Louis. So he picked an initial "E" because Joey is the traditional name of the clown.

could succeed in a medium which was less intimate than the night-club. He need not have worried. The Durante personality was to sweep the nation in whatever medium he turned to—vaudeville, musical comedy, motion pictures, radio, or television.

Another great comedian in the arena of after-dark entertainment was Joe E. Lewis, frequently described as "King of the Night Clubs."

Lewis originally set out as the fastest-talking comedian in Chicago. When he decided to change his nightclub job, he ran into the middle of a gangster feud which resulted in a brutal attack upon him by three strong-arm assailants. Newspaper headlines carried the story.

CABARET STAR'S THROAT SLASHED!
VICIOUS KNIFING SILENCES COMEDIAN!
JOE LEWIS STABBED, NEAR DEATH!

All the more tragic was the fact that in the attack, Joe's vocal cords had been damaged. It was years before the comedian was able to get about. But he courageously insisted upon his intention to return to the entertainment field. In a few years, the comedian rose from a hospital bed to become a nightclub entertainer whom the critics pronounced "a genius" and "one of the greatest." Joe's humor was largely in his gags.

"You'll notice that I'm doing a very fast show. I'm cutting out all the laughs," he'd say. Or: "These jokes may not sound like much to you but your laughs don't sound like much to me either." Or: "Everybody's breeding things. I crossed a rooster with a rooster—and got a very cross rooster."

With the close of theaters to traveling performers, the funny man had no place to show his comic skills, or so it seemed. The vaudeville acts that were on extended "vacation" found new audiences, vacationers in resort hotels. There were concentrations of people ready for a laugh or other entertainment. Frequently, they were city dwellers away from home in the country for a week or two. The Catskill Mountains, just outside of New York City, were dotted with hotels catering to old-country people and their children and grandchildren. The food and the humor often derived from old-country ways too.

To keep the customers happy, hotel owners hired spirited young men as waiters so that in their off hours they could amuse the

Dean Martin and Jerry Lewis were a successful laugh combination before they went their own separate ways. When they were on stage together, anything could happen.

Bert Lahr had his start in burlesque and vaudeville. His shows included Delmar's Revels, Hold Everything, *and* DuBarry Was a Lady.

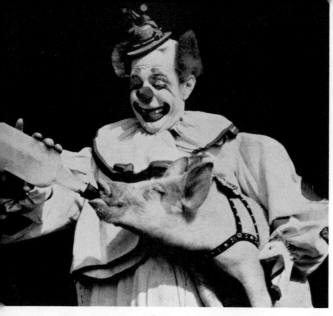

Felix Adler is a great modern whiteface clown. Some of the most famous former residents of "Clown Alley" have been Fred Stone, Red Skelton, Bobby Clark, Paul McCullough, Joe E. Brown.

guests. They organized activities, introduced people to each other, lead in singing, and entertained in the dining room or lodge in the hours after a family dinner. The waiters with comic flair tried out their material in one summer in one hotel and brought it to refinement or discarded it after retrial the following summer in another place. Some hotels competed to have name entertainers perform, but money was in short supply and there were plenty of aspiring performers to be had.

This was the borscht circuit, and it nourished many comics who later became popular in nightclubs, on radio, and on the stage. Among those pressed into service were Sid Caesar, Eddie Cantor, Henny Youngman, Morey Amsterdam, Milton Berle—the list could go on and on with names widely known later on. Lou Holtz, George Jessel, Buddy Hackett, Myron Cohn, and many others were in the tradition of the Jewish storyteller, with exaggerated style and large gestures designed to gain and keep the attention of the informal audiences.

In the late 1920s and early 1930s, the audiences became less sedate and more adult and discriminating. They were harsh judges, too, and even became hecklers. The comic learned to deal with interruptions, especially after the end of Prohibition when alcoholic drinks made people noisy. Many comics developed a line of insult humor which they used to put down interruptions. They wrote their own material, acted, danced, sang, and competed fiercely with one another.

Of course, there were many other talented stars who passed through the nightclub arena. These included Dean Martin and

Jerry Lewis, Joey Adams, Jerry Lester, Henny Youngman, Sophie Tucker, Jimmy Savo (originally a child-wonder juggler, he starred as rope-walker, dancer, singer, comedian and pantomimist), Danny Thomas and many others. Some of them are still in nightclub comedy.

During the same period when many comedians were going into the nightclubs, a new brand of comedian emerged into the bright sunlight—the baseball clown. There haven't been many of them, but they have represented a significant form of comedy.

Al Schacht and Nick Altrock were two baseball clowns who entertained millions of people in their day. Schacht's humor was largely pantomime, representing takeoffs of baseball stars, tennis players, boxers, and almost anyone who lent himself to physical satire.

Comedy and sports are traditional in America and you might say that the great American pastime is either telling jokes or playing ball. Many of our most popular Americans have either been comedians or ballplayers.

While the legitimate stage and the world of entertainment in general was carrying on, a gigantic firecracker was lit and spluttering, ready to go off with a boom.

Emmett Kelly, with broom instead of baseball bat, is providing comedy relief in the Big Leagues. One of the greatest circus clowns, Kelly was hired to provide comic entertainment for Brooklyn Dodger fans.

12

Funny Air

There was something wonderful about radio in the early days. A performer did not need to be beautiful. Nor dress well. You could even let down your suspenders and loosen your girdle while you were on the air.

Radio was the great equalizer. No matter how you looked, how much money you owned, how you dressed, it was only your voice that reached the people outside.

Of course, there still were those who thought radio was an interesting gadget but just couldn't see it as a commercial enterprise. For example, a widely respected advertising publication stated:

Any attempt to make the radio an advertising medium, in the accepted sense of the term, would, we think, prove positively offensive to great numbers of people. The family circle is not a public place, and advertising has no business intruding there unless it is invited. . . . The man who does not want to read a paint ad in the newspaper can turn the page and read something else. But the man at the end of the radio must listen, or shut it off entirely. That is a big distinction that ought not to be overlooked.

And, of course, in the early days, there were the same warnings from the diehards that had been sounded with the coming of the talking motion pictures. Listening to radio was supposed to be bad for the ears. To have a radio in the house, it was said, was a certain invitation to the starting of fires. But the number of radios being sold, despite their huge, ugly, bird-nest type of aerials and their myriad of expensive and mysterious tubes, continued to go up and up and up; and so did the ratings of some of the new radio stars who were to be heard weekly.

From the start it seems that radio comedians were favorites with the rapidly growing listening audience. Among the top scorers in popularity polls were Eddie Cantor, Fibber McGee and Molly, Ed Wynn, Jack Benny, Fred Allen, Edgar Bergen and Charlie McCarthy, Red Skelton, Amos 'n' Andy, Bob Hope, and Al Jolson.

Perhaps the most celebrated of radio's long list of outstanding funnymen was one who had the unique accomplishment of winning respect both from his fellow comedians and the general public—Fred Allen.

Allen, a former juggler from Boston, had a dry wit and a ready tongue and the ability to make up funny lines when he happened to have nothing written at the time. Commenting on the new medium of radio, Mr. Allen said: "Radio has the advantage over the theater. The show doesn't close if there's nobody in the balcony."

Quips from Fred Allen delighted the nation almost as much as those from the tongue or pen of Will Rogers a few years before.

Fred Allen and his "Allen's Alley" was a weekly Sunday night radio favorite.

Jack Benny established a national reputation as a penny-pincher, an egotist, and a man whose age seldom advanced. He drove an ancient Maxwell and was the rare comedian who was willing to make himself the butt of all the jokes.

Both men were natural descendants from the same stock—Jonathan of the early days of the American Yankee comedy.

"California," quipped Allen, "is a great place to live if you're an orange." Concerning company executives with whom he seemed to have a constant, though good-natured feud, Allen once said, "A vice president is a bit of executive fungus that falls on a desk that has been exposed to conference."

Because of his ad-libbing proclivities, Allen frequently found himself in hot water with the authorities. But censoring Allen wasn't always easy. He had a fast tongue as an ad libber and he knew his business. Once when a well-known sponsor was paying him a large salary, he made some biting reference to Scottish thrift. Several hundred Scotsmen from the Pittsburgh area signed an indignant letter saying that they did not intend ever again to use the product which the sponsor sold.

Since the product happened to be a laxative, Allen had no choice but to make his now-famous apology. "The prospect that they (the protesters) will go through life constipated so frightened the agency that they made me apologize."

Allen was very fearful that since the radio released such a huge number of machine-made jokes per night, it would dull the average person's responses. "Before radio," he said, "when a Will Rogers or a Peter Finley Dunne made a wisecrack, it would be quoted from one end of the country to the other and everyone repeated it for a month. Today, nobody remembers what I said on the radio last week, except some gag writers who are figuring ways to steal the jokes."

One of the most amusing of Fred Allen's radio programs was his famous "Allen's Alley" in which he would go from door to door weekly, interviewing three or four carefully developed personalities. Included were Mrs. Nussbaum, played by Minerva Pious; Senator Claghorn, the noisy politician from the Deep South, played by Kenny Delmar; Titus Moody, the New England farmer, played by Parker Fennelly; and the Irishman Ajax Cassidy, played by Peter Donald.

While Fred Allen radiated a satirical, sharp self-confidence, his friendly archrival, Jack Benny, was the personification of something quite different. As a matter of fact, Benny made a living both on radio and television perfecting the fine art of self-humiliation. Someone had said that Jack Benny would outlast all the other comedians because he had one tremendous advantage: he didn't have to do anything. There is some belief that Benny brought more laughs to more people than any other entertainer who ever lived. His type of performance involved perfect timing as one of his major accomplishments.

Through the years he built up an entire characterization of Jack Benny as a stingy, vainglorious, gulled, and tyrannized individual who pinched his pennies, whose bark was always more dangerous than his bite, and whose age was always a source of painful sensitivity to him.

His technique, which lasted him through his many years in the entertainment world, was never to punch too hard so that, should

Jack Benny, center, with band leader Phil Harris, and Eddie Anderson, the "Rochester" of radio and television fame.

Charles Correll and Freeman Gosden originally went on the air in a Sam 'n' Henry *skit. In 1928, they began their* Amos 'n' Andy *program and soon became a national comedy situation.*

some of his lines fall by the wayside without laughter, the audience seldom knew the difference.

Jack Benny was one of the first performers on the radio to have laughs turned on himself, the star of the program. He developed the character of the man with human frailties. As a matter of fact, he made a career out of developing these human frailties and making them known to millions of people all over the country.

Explaining the humor of his program, Benny once said, "I'm a big shot, see? I'm fast-talking. I'm a smart guy. I'm boasting about how marvelous I am. I am a marvelous lover. I'm a marvelous fiddle player. Then five minutes after I start shooting off my mouth, my cast makes a schmo out of me. Wherever I go, whatever I do, I get into trouble for no good reason at all."

Never pushing, never aggressive, the Benny style goes something like this:

> Here it is seven days until Christmas and I hate to admit it, but I haven't even begun to do my Christmas shopping. I guess because it's always such a problem for me. There are so many people I have to remember, close associates, Don Wilson, Dennis Day . . . and then there's Rochester. Now, Rochester has been working for me for eighteen years and it's so hard to know what to get him . . . he's got nothing. And Don Wilson . . . there at least I got some help. His wife told me he would like a shirt. She told me his size, 16–33. Now where are you going to find a shirt with a 33 neck and a 16 sleeve? . . . Then there are the boys in my orchestra. Of course, I always exchange gifts with them. And they've already given me mine. They sent me a beautiful five-carat diamond ring. Now there was no card in the gift or anything, but I knew it was from the boys in the orchestra when the police came and took it back. Fortunately, in our next musical arrangement the clarinet player has a ten-year

The beloved husband-and-wife team of Fibber Mc-Gee and Molly played on the radio for many years by Marian and Jim Jordan.

rest. Anyway, the ring does count as a gift so I have to reciprocate. Now on Christmas I usually give Frankie Remley, my guitar player, a bottle of bourbon. But this year his doctor absolutely refuses to let him have any liquor . . . so I got Remley something else. He was just thrilled. I gave him the name of a new doctor. . . .

Bob Hope, one of the talented young comedians who became a national figure as a result of radio, based a large part of his comedy approach on his careful timing, just like Jack Benny. And, like Benny, Hope also used self-ridicule as a means of getting laughs. If every joke he made about the size of his nose paid off in money, he could afford to have his nose fixed many times over.

One of the first things that Hope learned in the entertainment field was patience: "One of the things I learned was to have courage to wait," Hope stated. "I'd stand there waiting for them to get it (the joke) for a long time, longer than any other comedian

Ed Wynn as the Fire Chief. Wynn was the first radio star to insist that a live audience be present for his broadcasts.

had enough guts to wait. My idea was to let them know who was running things."

Thus, Hope would crack a joke—on the stage, on radio, or on television—and bravely wait it out until the very interlude of waiting became almost a national symbol for hilarity.

Hope had a reputation in some circles for being a mere repeater of gag chatter written by his ghosts. Whether this was true or not, he perfected his manner of presenting lines and became an institution. A sample of his radio comedy monologue indicates the general type of humor which made Hope famous:

I'm a little tired tonight. I'm building a new house in North Hollywood and I want to tell you that's hard work. I think I'll have to hire a carpenter to help me. It's one of those California all-weather houses . . . you know, six rooms, a big sun porch . . . and a direct wire to the coast guard! I decided to build a permanent home now that I am doing pretty well in pictures. Of course, it's the only house on the block with wheels on it, but I'm really putting up a nice house. The other day when the lumber came in . . . the termites were standing around smacking their lips and applauding. You'll like the inside of the house. It's really got a beautiful bathroom . . . when you want cold water, all you have to do is dig . . .

Edgar Bergen and his wooden-headed partner Charlie McCarthy, a ventriloquist act that had all radio-listening America laughing. When Charlie was made mascot of the Chicago White Sox, he remarked, "some of my relatives are bats."

There have been many comedy teams in the entertainment world, but none more successful in radio than George Burns and Gracie Allen. Many of their old films can be seen on television.

when you want hot water, you just go deeper! It's got three guest rooms . . . the green room, the blue room, and the jade room. It's really all the same room . . . we just change the lights for the first two and burn incense for the other! And I've got a new idea in the bedroom . . . the walls just pull out from a bed. I have a Murphy bed and a Morris chair in my room, the room is so small. The other morning Murphy woke up with an accent!

While this type of humor may not seem complex, the art of being a stand-up comedian is not an easy one. Hope developed from a hoofer (dance routine) into a gag man. Part of his success was his ability to study his audience and to angle his jokes to fit the mood or background or current events of a given situation.

Another pioneer of early radio was Ed Wynn (The Perfect Fool), who had achieved an enviable reputation as a comedian in burlesque and on the musical comedy stage. When he took to radio, Wynn achieved even greater popularity as the famous "Fire Chief." Wynn was the first of the great comedians to broadcast from a stage with an actual admission-paying audience. The practice became standard after a time and has helped many comedians establish rapport with their audiences, something badly needed for laugh making. Commenting upon the contrast between his legitimate stage activity and the radio, Ed Wynn said ruefully, "I spent $750,000 publicizing myself as the Perfect Fool. And almost overnight it is forgotten and I am known only as the Fire Chief."

Although Jimmy Durante had been a star in nightclub and

Gertrude Berg as Mollie in "The Goldbergs" has a unique position of love in the hearts of radio and television audiences.

Colonel Lemuel Q. Stoopnagle and Bud Hulich, known familiarly to radio audiences as Stoopnagle and Bud.

legitimate stage, with the coming of radio he teamed up with young Garry Moore to become a sensational success on the new medium. Garry's ability to ad lib was a great asset in his teaming up with Durante since Jimmy himself was unpredictable and needed a fast-stepping partner to keep up with him.

It was on the radio that Jimmy made nationally popular some of his famous songs. It was on the radio that his "Good night, Mrs. Calabash, wherever you are," first became familiar to millions of people.

Many stars brightened the early radio days and actually became national institutions for many years. Fibber McGee and Molly became family favorites as did the Goldbergs, featuring

Gertrude Berg. There were, of course, Amos 'n' Andy, the Happiness Boys, Burns and Allen, Stoopnagle and Budd, Eddie Cantor, and Henry Morgan.

Even Will Rogers took to the air, and his impersonation of President Calvin Coolidge caused much confusion nationally. Rogers had designed his imitation to be an obvious joke, but so many people were deceived by it that he was forced to apologize for the impersonation.

Household radio grew to such an extent that almost everyone had a set. Most people unconsciously blessed the fact that they could listen to music or to a comedian and at the same time use their eyes for other things—cooking, homework, reading, writing letters.

But the reign of the Ear was not to last forever. The almighty Eye was to have its day—and soon.

Bob and Ray, two men of madness and mirth, are really Bob Elliot and Ray Goulding. They started as disc jockeys and developed a fresh brand of humor on radio and later on television.

The Ritz Brothers (Al, Jimmy, and Harry) were a successful radio combination.

13

Now You See It

"Television is nothing like vaudeville," Fred Allen once commented. "In vaudeville you had one act and a constantly changing audience—TV, like radio, is just the opposite. You have the same audience all the time, so the act must be changed after each performance. Naturally, the quality of the material gets low."

Jim Bishop, biographer of the comedian, Jackie Gleason, wrote:

> Television is the most perpetually baffling invention since the one-way street. It is, in one breath, the savior of actors and their executioners. It creates and it kills.
>
> A man may work for months or years to draw up a good animal act. In the days of vaudeville he could tour the country for two years or more, at $125 a week, without ever meeting the same audience twice.
>
> Today he puts his act on a television network show and, in six minutes, he has been seen by fifty million persons, has earned $500, and his act is finished. It cannot be shown again. Theatrically, he is dead.

Comedians were not slow in expressing their feelings about the new medium.

"When the lumber barons went through a forest," Sid Caesar said, "they took everything they wanted and didn't bother to reseed or to heal the leftover trees that were hurt by exposure to the elements. Then came a law correcting this. TV has no such law. It should. The networks have gone through the forests of comedians, and they have done nothing to replace them or to help the old stars fight exposure."

Milton Berle, the first casualty of television, began his career by play-
ing in some fifty films without a comedy line in any of them. He rose
through vaudeville, musical comedy, and Ziegfeld Follies and was the
first big-name comedian to appear on TV. In 1948, he became known as
"Mr. Television." "His programs," commented The New Yorker, "are
said to have so powerful a hold on the TV public that shopkeepers who
would ordinarily be open for business between eight and nine on Tues-
day evenings now close down their stores for lack of customers."

Bert Lahr developed his comedy talent from the early burlesque, vaudeville, and musical comedy. "There is no place today
for comedians to develop," he said. "There is no burlesque, no
vaudeville. Just a few clubs and television."

Ed Wynn believed that it was dangerous to have the network
and advertising experts sit in judgment on the comedian. "Being
a comedian is an art and not a business. It should not be judged
exclusively by business standards."

"The industry seems to wear many of the comics out and to cut
off the progress of newcomers before they have a fair chance to
develop," Steve Allen commented.

Lou Holtz, a popular comedian of the 1930s, said: "You can't
stay successful every week as a comedian. . . . Al Jolson was
the greatest . . . but remember this. The people out of town saw
him, at the most, about three times a year. When he arrived in
Minneapolis or Seattle or any place else, it was a big event. I'm
pretty sure if Jolson sang and clowned for them on television
every Wednesday night, by the time he went into his second or
third year, they'd be turning him off."

Red Buttons was a promising young comedian when he entered TV. "Red had definite talent," said one TV executive. "It seems he just ran out of gas. He was good for one big season, but he had a limited amount of tricks to last in this business. . . ."

Sam Levenson, another comedian with a serious approach, pointed out: "Great jokes don't grow on trees. Great jokes have to ripen. TV burns up subject matter faster than it can often be produced."

Harold Lloyd asked whether the weekly pace was to blame. "We used to produce a two-reel silent comedy every week, month after month," Lloyd recalled. "And they were funny and did not seem to run out of material. True, we often used to scratch our heads and wonder what we would use for gags. But we managed somehow. And the public didn't seem to tire of them. . . . We never knew from day to day or hour to hour what we would do to bring the laughs. Most of our humor was spontaneous and without written scripts."

The influential magazine *Advertising Age* joined the discussion:

> There are no training grounds left for young comics. Gone is the classic burlesque, the Chautauqua circuit, vaudeville, radio, movies, revue in the legitimate theatre, or any of the try-out places. Television has, ironically enough, wiped out these old starting gates.

In an article, "Clowns in Decline," the *New York Times* observed in 1957, "After thirty years of unchallenged dominance it now seems generally conceded that comedians no longer are the mainstay of broadcasting. The inexorable law of overexposure has caught up with the majority of clowns."

The history of comedy shows that the great comedians, while often using the same routine, entered creatively into every performance. Whether it was Joseph Jefferson in *Rip Van Winkle*, a Weber and Fields revue, or the Marx Brothers in *Coconuts*, the performance was never exactly the same. Audiences would return again and again to see the same show. A creative process was at work which made each performance different no matter how often seen.

On TV the "ad lib" was—in a period of teleprompters, memorized scripts, ghost writers, and vast audiences—considered a foolhardy risk. Even those who could ad lib and who were fast

"I just take what I see and exaggerate it a little bit," said Sid Caesar. *"I pick out the obvious things that everybody is familiar with but never stops to think about."*

on their mental feet often rehearsed their ad libs to make certain that they did not say something which might offend not just a theater full of people, but the entire nation.

Small wonder that the genuine ad lib became so rare as to be almost nonexistent!

In the late 1950s, the use of parody, satire, and critical comment as source material for comedy was almost as rare as the genuine ad lib.

The *New York Times* remarked in 1957 on this situation that, "this is evidently no time for comedy, unless it is an amiable jest about family foibles or a report on the war between the sexes. Things used to be different. Authors could poke . . . fun at politics, business and babbitry in all its aspects. . . ."

But whatever the reason for the decline of American comedians or comedy, history gave confidence that the decline would be short-lived. Comedy is a persistent commodity. Discouraged or suppressed in one medium, it springs up again in another—at a later date.

Art Carney and Jackie Gleason, from a scene in "The Honeymooners," for many years one of television's most popular "situation comedies."

But it was not until the 1960s that there was a rebirth of the comic spirit.

As comedians disappeared from TV screens in homes all over America, Westerns and TV programs featuring violence and crime increased. Gagsters were displaced by gangsters and, for change of pace, there was professional wrestling and sex.

Of course, television was not the only communications medium with a paralyzed funny bone. Radio went the way of its kid brother, TV, only more so. Movies, for the most part, forgot how to be funny.

Generally, the movement of comedians in the late 1950s was away from TV and toward Broadway. People like Lucille Ball, Wally Cox, George Gobel, Phil Silvers, Art Carney, Sid Caesar, Imogene Coca, and Milton Berle only occasionally returned to TV during this era.

"I've done a lot of TV work this year," quipped Berle in a nightclub appearance. "I fixed two sets yesterday."

Danny Kaye, Bob Hope, and Victor Borge used TV appearances sparingly, only appearing in specials occasionally.

Borge, a comedian of top rank, was particularly careful not to outlive his TV welcome; he appeared only once or twice a year. Some people, he stated, "always insist on something new. They force the humorist to overexpose himself. . . . If what the performer possesses is valuable, it shouldn't be changed for change's sake. Let him repeat his best stuff. Let new generations see it."

More and more professional comedians turned to serious acting, with various degrees of success. Jackie Gleason, described as "the most celebrated buffoon ever to rise through United States television," did so well as a serious motion picture actor that it won him a *Time* magazine cover portrait.

Panel shows gave a few comedians, such as Groucho Marx and Henry Morgan, a chance to be funny. But here the comedian tended to be more the stand-up (or sit-down) comedian than the traditional laughmaker.

Dick Van Dyke, like Ed Wynn, used physical comedy to provoke laughter.

The talented mimic and comic character actor, Sid Caesar, confided to friends: "I think I'm at the end of the line, I've had it." He told the columnist, Erskine Johnson: "The lawyers and the accountants were starting to take television away from the creators. They wanted me to go on film and they talked about residuals and spin-offs, and reruns and capital gains, and how you can sell the reruns and the spin-offs. They wanted shows with shock treatment, not truth."

Some comedians found the going easier in TV's situation comedies. Here, Mom, Pop, and the kids (or some variation of them) were often the central figures. Professional comedians often become actors and actresses speaking lines written by gag writers.

The modern TV situation comedy received its first big push in the 1950s with Lucille Ball's "I Love Lucy" series. Testimony to her comic style was the continued showing of that series over a period of more than twenty years and before a new generation of viewers.

Other classic situation comedies of the era included the notable Phil Silvers as "Sergeant Bilko," the "Dick Van Dyke Show," and the "Honeymooners" with Jackie Gleason and Art Carney, Audrey Meadows and Joyce Randolph. The situation comedy made it easier for the comedian to survive on TV than any other regularly scheduled form.

Among the few who survived in "traditional" comedy was Red Skelton. He featured a pantomime character called Freddie the Free Loader, who was in the Jonathan tradition.

Lucille Ball won national television acclaim in both her "I Love Lucy" and "The Lucy Show" series. She began her dramatic work at the age of fifteen, appearing on Broadway and then Hollywood where she first served as a chorus girl.

Bob Newhart

There was at first some question as to whether a physical comedian like Skelton, depending so much on his body movement and acrobatics, could succeed on TV. Perhaps Skelton's success developed from the fact that he was a happy clown in the tragic era of the '60s. This was the time of the assassination of youthful President John F. Kennedy and the continuing war in southeast Asia.

Jack Benny was another durable comedian who appeared to defy the trend. One young comic, marveling at Benny's longevity, commented: "He can get people laughing just by standing there and looking at someone."

Comedians like Skelton and Benny established such a bond of understanding between themselves and their audiences—a sort of lovers' pact—that they seemed able to defy the high mortality rate of TV exposure.

But new comedians were in the wings waiting to take the stage.

Nichols and May

The 1960s witnessed a rebirth of the comic spirit, but few people could have guessed the exact form the new laughmakers were to assume.

Among these newcomers was Carol Burnett, perhaps the single happiest answer of her sex to the drought of laughmakers. Coming to the front via the Garry Moore TV Show, Miss Burnett gained the laughs and affections of millions by a welcome combination of irreverence for pomp and versatility of talent.

Miss Burnett originally came to New York from the West Coast; she had her eyes set on the stage. But given a chance by Moore, she soon became a TV fixture. Evidently doing what came naturally, she combined athletics, clowning, songs, and dances. Her humor, above all else, was a determined foe of fraud.

As Neal Gilkyson Stuart pointed out in *The Ladies' Home Journal*: "If she wears a pretty dress, she confides, 'And I *smell* divine!', thus ruining the perfumed guile. If she wears a wig, it is invariably snatched off, revealing her own flattened hair beneath. Every crafty thought, base motive, ache or hangover and trembling hope is so pitiably naked that it commands excruciating sympathy.

" 'You are never going to forget tonight!' exclaims the handsome man as he lets her into his apartment.

" 'I'm not?' she gasps hopefully, and in two words she exposes the poor palpitating heart of the healthy, lonely female. . . ."

When Jack Benny invited Miss Burnett to take part in a Tarzan-Jane TV routine on his television program, her first words were: "Gee, can I play Jane?"

Another bright comic following time-tested laugh-making practices was the pliable Dick Van Dyke. That comedy pro from Sid Caesar's "Show of Shows," Carl Reiner, conceived the "Dick Van Dyke Show," wrote many of its scripts, was a consultant when he was not writing them, and even slipped into some of the acts as a bit actor.

The show's supporting cast was well chosen. There was veteran comedian Morey Amsterdam, present when television comedy was born; his partner, the former baby star of radio, Rose Marie; and Mary Tyler Moore, who proved again that good looks need not be a barrier to good laugh making.

One explanation of the Van Dyke success was the comedian's link with sound comic tradition. "I am a visual, physical come-

Mort Sahl

dian," Van Dyke said, "I still hate to get up alone. People think
I'm a stand-up comic. I'm not."

Inspection of the Van Dyke show revealed the descent from
vigorous traditional American comedy. There was a live audience,
as Mary Tyler Moore put it, "to tell us where the jokes are."

Van Dyke could take a pratfall with the best of the old timers, and there was a spontaneous quality reminiscent of Mack
Sennett days. "Some of our funniest shows have come from our
worst scripts," Van Dyke said.

Other laughmakers of the early 1960s carrying forward comic
traditions included Jack E. Leonard, the veteran king of the "insult" comedians. Leonard was in the tradition of old burlesque-
vaudeville laughmakers, often depending more on native wit and
the ability to ad lib humorous lines than on gag writers.

Shelley Berman
All "standup" or "sit down
on a stove" comedians
brought a rebirth of satire.

There were many who laughed harder at Victor Borge's rare television "concerts" than at any other comedy act.

Jerry Lewis was a popular comedian, one of the few laughmakers of the era able to attract large audiences to motion picture theaters. Although he leaned heavily on the obvious for his laughs, Lewis was essentially a physical comedian. Another was Buddy Hackett, the heavy-set, rubbery-faced funnyman, whose questionable grammar hid a quick wit. A fellow comedian said of Hackett: "Buddy knows how to use his body and his face more than most comedians today."

A notable comic innovator was Ernie Kovacs, whose death early in 1962 shocked the entertainment-loving nation. An advocate of zany sketches and wild gags, Kovacs constantly reached for ever wilder comic situations in his TV shows. Impatient with trying

Carol Burnett was one of the few comediennes who was consistently able to challenge male funnymen on the popularity scale.

to fit old motion picture or radio techniques into the relatively new medium of television, Kovacs believed in experimentation. "There isn't anything that you can't make fun of if you want to," he said.

His humor was largely visual. He even began to produce complete TV shows entirely in pantomime, the only sound being classical music carefully selected to fit the mood of what he was trying to say. Under Kovacs' spell, painted portraits spoke; the water in a painted waterfall gurgled; a duck in a shooting gallery produced a gun from under its wing and shot back; a tense operating room closeup became, as the camera rolled back, a family carving a turkey.

In a commercial for a cigar company, Kovacs participated in a typical cowboy gun fight. After the shooting, he lit one of his huge cigars. Smoke poured out of him as though from a sieve.

Kovacs was one of the first comedians of the period who could be called a pioneer. He was not to be the last. As the 1960s developed, comedy increasingly reflected the need for topical comment and reaction to events of the day.

Among the influences that helped encourage younger comedians were TV "host" programs. Ed Sullivan, who almost single-handedly kept old-fashioned vaudeville abreast of the machine age, gave innumerable comedians their big chance. The Jack Paar TV show gave a helping hand to scores of laughmakers including Dick Gregory, Jack Carter, Hermione Gingold, Phyllis Diller, Nipsey Russell, Dody Goodman, Joey Bishop, Milt Kamen, Buddy Hackett, Dave Astor, Jonathan Winters, Cliff Arquette (Charlie Weaver), and Alan King.

Comedians like Jackie Gleason sometimes turned to serious shows when comedy work was not available.

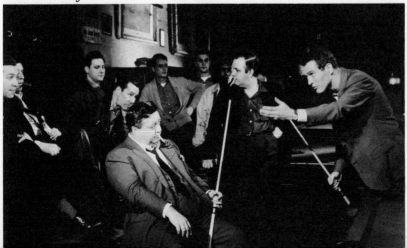

Paar himself tended to be more a master of ceremonies than a professional funnyman. "Absolute honesty is important," Paar was quoted by *Television Magazine*. "Someone who is unreal, phony, shows through. You might fool the viewers once or twice, but you can't fool them for long."

In an era of prepared scripts and frozen fun, Paar provided a rather welcome feeling of spontaneity. The human quality showed through more frequently on Paar's programs than on most others. And people seemed hungry for it. They may have accounted for the amazing fact that Paar accumulated on his late TV show some 164 participating television stations and a viewing audience approaching 3,000,000 steady followers with some 8,633,000 at peak.

Another skilled and sophisticated entertainer who pioneered as combined comedian and host was Steve Allen, who helped introduce scores of funnymen including Louis Nye, Bill Dana, the Smothers Brothers, Joey Forman, Tom Poston, Mort Sahl, and Don Knotts.

Still another pioneer was low-keyed Dave Garroway, who for years woke people up on the "Today" show. "Don't tell lies to the people," was the way Garroway once explained his success. "If somebody doesn't show up, say he isn't here. If something goes wrong, admit it."

In the years that followed, successors to hosts such as Garroway and Paar were numerous: Merv Griffin, Joey Bishop, Johnny Carson, Dick Cavett, David Frost, Mike Douglas, and more. Some served as part-time comedians. Others contributed to comedy by giving young, aspiring laughmakers their chance. Almost every comedian to come forward in this era was either born or developed on one or all of these "talk" shows.

While television has presented numerous comic talents—some with short lives, others more long lasting—many people say that the most spectacular is Woody Allen. Starting as a gag writer for newspaper columnists while he was struggling through high school in Brooklyn, Woody earned a good amount of money letting other people take credit for his zany jokes. He was not the first comedy writer to stand on the footlight side of the stage, but some aspects of his comic style and personality were unique. He appeared as a guest on late night TV shows, out of season for more important people. He reminded people of the kid next door who seemed to be a loser, shy, reluctant to enter the competition.

What a surprise when Woody developed what seemed spontaneous humor and showed himself as a zany winner in many of life's toughest situations. Beneath this slightly balding, fading red head was a hard-working, intelligent man, who combined a lovable personality with a soaring imagination. He wrote his own material for TV and clubs; and he wrote, acted in, and directed his own movies.

As Woody developed, he changed his style, until in his full-length movies, he touched on serious issues and political absurdities which were a far cry from his beginnings in small nightclubs.

During this period, TV variety shows were not the only vehicle giving comedians an opportunity to be funny in public. There was also a rebirth of popularity of the old-fashioned phonograph record—unbreakable, long playing, and of high fidelity.

According to Paul Kresh, a member of the National Academy of Recording Arts and Sciences, in the *American Record Guide*: "The growing list of comics on discs makes one wonder at times if they've all abandoned the borscht circuit, nightclubs and TV channels for recording studios in order to preserve their art for posterity.

"They haven't, of course, and moreover they tend to bring these backgrounds right along with them. Some are subtle, some crass

Steve Allen helped introduce many young comics to television audiences. Included was an offbeat team known as the Smothers Brothers.

and vulgar, some cruel, some whimsical, some 'sick'; some understate, most overstate, and a few are just downright, indefinably funny."

W. Schwann, Inc., publisher of the widely used long playing record catalogue, points out that prior to 1960 it did not even include a special category of comedy records. The first listing included ninety-six records. The following year, in 1961, the number had jumped to 284, while in 1963 there were no less than 450 titles. The number rose steadily throughout the decade. By the end of the 1960s the most productive comedy disc makers included: Moms Mabley, Homer & Jethro, Dewey Pigmeat Markham, Jonathan Winters, Brother Dave Gardner, Allan Sherman, the Smothers Brothers, Bill Cosby, Lenny Bruce, Shelley Berman, and Phyllis Diller.

Credit for the first hit comedy record of this decade generally is given to Andy Griffith, direct descendant of the Jonathan, country bumpkin type of comedian, whose *What It Was, Was Football* deserves rating both as a laugh classic and a pioneer. Other early discs include Stan Freburg's *St. George and the Dragonet* and Eddie Lawrence's recording.

Comedy records were not exactly new. Edison's *Uncle Josh* series was popular decades ago as was Victor's famous *Cohen on the Telephone*. The comedians Moran and Mack, the *Two Black Crows*, made records that were big sellers. However, nothing has occurred in history that can equal the tremendous surge in popularity of the comedy records which started in the '60s. Records of Bob Newhart or Bill Dana (Jose Jiminez) were listed right up there with the records of Frank Sinatra, Harry Belafonte, and Mitch Miller.

Most people didn't know Bob Newhart existed until a phonograph record with his thin, nasal voice and his brand of subtle satire began to sell by the thousands in communities all over America.

Included among his best-known routines was an Abraham Lincoln sequence. This was an imaginary telephone conversation between Lincoln and his press agent. Basically, it's the idea, Newhart explained, that if we had "today's science of advertising during the Civil War, and there was no Lincoln around, an ad man would have created a Lincoln out of whoever was in office. And he'd say things (in a one-way telephone conversation) like this":

Hi, ya, sweetheart, how's everything going? How was Gettysburg? Abe, listen, I got your note, what seems to be the problem? You're thinking of shaving it off? Abe, you're kidding, aren't you? Don't you see that that's part of the image? It's right, with a shawl, and a stovepipe hat. You don't have a shawl? Where did you leave the shawl this time, Abe? You left it in Washington? What are you wearing, Abe? A cardigan. Abe, don't you see that that doesn't fit with a stovepipe hat . . . Abe, trust in us on this—that's what you're paying us for. Abe, you got the speech? You haven't changed the speech, have you, Abe? Abe, why do you change the speeches? You typed it? Abe, how many times have we told you on the backs of envelopes, it will look ad lib, as if you wrote it on the way over. Abe, do the speech the way Charlie wrote it. The inaugural address won. Will you do it the way he wrote it? You talked to some newspaper men? I wish you wouldn't talk to newspaper men. You're always putting your foot—No, no, no, that is just what I am driving at, Abe, you're a railsplitter before you were an attorney. Abe, read the biography again.

Like many of the new comedians of the 1960s, Newhart had serious thoughts behind his comedy lines. In an interview by Pete Martin in *The Saturday Evening Post*, Newhart said:

"Those who control the medium are obsessed with the notion that if they offend even one viewer, they have one less customer. What the TV biggies don't know is that people like entertainment with bite. They want satire. The growth of talking-record sales proves that."

Another phenomenally successful laughmaker on records was the team of Mike Nichols and Elaine May, who began as cabaret comedians. Highly gifted, they observed life about them and composed devastating satirical routines to expose folly and hypocrisy. "The role of the writer or artist is to be the competent observer," they said.

Steve Allen gave Nichols and May a chance on his TV program. The team was a hit. They exposed to laughs the frailties and frauds they found, whether it was the overzealous mother who would not eat for days for fear her mouth would be full when her son called; the dentist who confessed his love for his patient; the name-dropping disc jockey who knew Bertrand Russell well; or the male patient who visited a lady doctor for the first time.

Allan Sherman and Vaughn Meader were two more successful comedians who recorded at that time. Sherman was at first a creator of laugh-making material for others, such as Joe E. Lewis and Jackie Gleason. Respected as an ingenious "comedy brain," Sherman helped dream up an idea for a TV panel show in 1951. "I've Got A Secret" ran for years.

He tried on his own stuff just for size, and usually before small groups of friends. Known as a satirical funnyman in Hollywood circles, Sherman was not widely recognized until a Warner Brothers representative heard him put on his guitar song routine at a private party.

My Son, the Folk Singer resulted. Sherman used both his typewriter and his guitar, putting irreverent new lyrics to beloved old melodies. His first *My Son* record quickly sold a million and zoomed to the top of the record hit parade. A sequel, *My Son, the Celebrity*, was also gobbled up by a public hungry for this kind of sophisticated humor.

If Sherman's records sold amazingly well, Vaughn Meader's laugh making about the Kennedy family sold even better. People rushed to their nearest record store, demanding Meader's discs in such numbers that they had to be rationed.

For ten years Shelley Berman tried unsuccessfully to get a foothold in the serious theater. Then he turned to comedy. A success-

Jack Benny pictured before the junior high school that bears his name, built in Waukegan, Illinois, his birthplace.

Bob Hope, the wealthiest comedian in history, received an honorary degree at Georgetown University in 1962. His advice to young people about to go out into the world was: "Don't go."

ful appearance on Jack Paar's show helped send him on his way. In rapid succession came engagements at the Blue Angel in New York and then twelve shows for Ed Sullivan. Shelley became a household name. His recording, *Inside Shelley Berman*, sold in the hundreds of thousands and was the first nonmusical album to be awarded the Gold Record.

Berman, who has helped open the record field for comedians, also blazed a trail for them on the concert stage. Traveling by plane, train, and car, he covered hundreds of thousands of miles on three concert tours which attracted huge crowds in every section of the country. On one tour playing in twenty-seven cities, he set a mark for all to shoot at in one run of four performances at the Purdue University Field House in Lafayette, Indiana, where 26,435 people paid to see him. He was the first nonmusical performer ever to appear at Chicago's famed Orchestra Hall.

Berman found comedy in ordinary frustrations of life about him: a telephone conversation with a child who keeps hanging up the phone, television commercials, a dentist ominously taking x-rays, the smile of an airline stewardess.

"I don't think it is my job to make a social comment," Berman once said. "If a social comment comes out of what I do, that's gravy. But it is not what I am after . . . I am after laughs."

If Shelley Berman was not primarily interested in social comment, another comedian, Mort Sahl, who gained fame in the early '60s, was. Sahl was characterized as "one of the earliest ripples in the wave of cerebral American comics." Asked how he makes people laugh, Sahl answered: "I tell the truth and the people break up."

Of course, it was not quite that simple. Called the "thinking man's comedian," Sahl combined irreverence with a willingness to tread little-walked paths in the area of topical comment.

Sahl was innately controversial; a one-man reaction to the period of the mid-1950s, when noncomformity was sometimes considered subversive. As a matter of fact, the joke that set Sahl off on his nightclub career had to do with a coat he described as a "McCarthy jacket."

"It is like an Eisenhower jacket," he quipped, "except it has an extra zipper to go across the mouth."

His usual finish punch line in his monologues was the question, "Are there any groups that I have not offended?"

His technique was, as he said, a sort of flowing free association of ideas, carelessly (it would seem) linked together, but actually interconnected with considerable care and artistry.

Sahl began in the West Coast nightclub, the hungry i, and then moved to TV and recordings. He had the knack of amusing people in both high and low positions. Adlai Stevenson's appreciation of his quips was said to have helped rocket Sahl to prominence. Political leaders of all parties laughed at Sahl, although more Democrats laughed than Republicans.

Buddy Hackett said of Sahl that he was "not sick, he's aggressive." And aggressive he was. *The New Yorker* magazine once stated that Sahl was "against practically everything." Actually, Sahl disputed this, saying: "If I criticize somebody, it's only because I have higher hopes for the world, something good to replace the bad."

Another comedian of the new type and new era was Dick Gregory. A sit-down or stand-up, cigarette-smoking comedian out of Chicago, Gregory was sometimes referred to as "the black Mort Sahl."

"In the Congo," replied Gregory, "Mort Sahl would be referred to as the white Dick Gregory!"

At the beginning of his career, Gregory washed cars during the day to augment his show business income. His rise to fame was one of the sensational successes of the entertainment industry. Gregory also depended on the day's news for ammunition, carefully studying newspapers and magazines before each performance.

The story is that Gregory made his first major appearance in

Peter Sellers

Phil Silvers

Buddy Hackett

Mickey Rooney

Carl Reiner

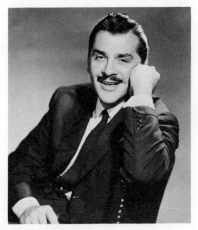

Ernie Kovacs

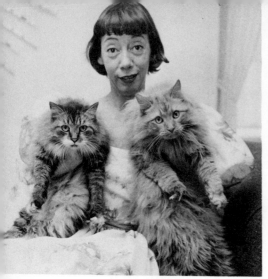

Imogene Coca

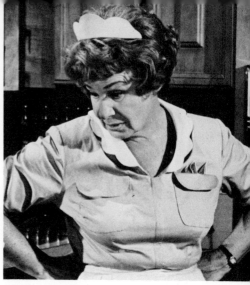

Shirley Booth

the Playboy Club in Chicago when the main comedian failed to show up. That evening a convention of businesss executives from the South was present. There was some hesitation before Gregory was permitted to go on.

He began something like this:

> Ladies and gentlemen, I understand there are a good many Southerners in the room tonight. I know the South very well. I spent twenty years there one night. . . . It is dangerous for me to go back. You see . . . when I drink I think I am Polish. . . . One night, I got so drunk I moved out of my own neighborhood. . . . The last time I was down South, I walked into this restaurant and this waitress came up to me and said, "We don't serve colored people in here," "That's all right," I said, "I don't eat them, bring me a whole fried chicken instead."

Martha Raye

Jackie Leonard

Henry Morgan

Tony Randall

When he was finished, so the story goes, the audience rose in applause and several members invited him South to entertain their friends.

Gregory had a sly humor which sneaked up on the listener when least expected: "The way things are . . . ten years from now, you'll have to be my color to get a job. . . . I am really for Abraham Lincoln. If it hadn't been for Abe, I would still be on the open market. . . . I sat at a lunch counter for nine months. They finally integrated and didn't have what I wanted. . . .

"They are making a picture called Stagecoach South. . . . They offered me the leading part and I turned it down, because I know the first time they make a Negro Western, the Indians gonna win. . . . When I do land on the moon, a six-legged, green-skinned man is sure to come up and tell me he don't want me marrying his sister."

Hermione Gingold   Sam Levenson

Jerry Lewis

Gregory invaded the Southland in 1963 to lend the influence of his name on the side of people demonstrating for equality. In Greenwood, Mississippi, the United Press International reported, "Police manhandled comedian Dick Gregory when he and other Negroes refused orders to disperse a voter registration march to the voting booths."

In Birmingham, Alabama, a few weeks later, Gregory again joined demonstrators for equal rights and was jailed with a large number of others including hundreds of children.

"We're glad this city doesn't have enough jails or enough police brutality to go around," Gregory commented from jail. "There are all kinds of hunting licenses and seasons for wild game," he said, "but it's open season on us—Negroes—24 hours a day."

Dick Nolan in the *San Francisco Examiner* claimed at the time that Gregory was a double-edged disappointment. "He is a disappointment to the hot-eyed radicals of the left. He is a disappointment to the cold-hearted radicals of the right. But to an American thirsting for laughs, Gregory 'represents a new voice' in the ranks of comedians—the first major Negro laughmaker since Bert Williams."

In a few brief years, a changing Dick Gregory was to herald a dramatic change in much of American comedy.

14

The Comedian: Barometer of National Health

In the 1970s, comedy increasingly became an instrument of political and social commentary.

Certainly not all funnymen turned to current events for ammunition. Many—among them Red Skelton, Lucille Ball, Jerry Lewis, Jack Benny, and Jimmy Durante—continued comedy as usual. "Songs is my forty," said Jimmy. "Wid a couple a jokes, a couple a gals in da act—what else am I gonna do? Best t'ing for me is to jest be me."

But numerous laughmakers were finding popularity, particularly among youth, in a "comedy of dissent." According to Steve Allen, "There is a generation of angry young men. Youth is revolting all over the world, and all the world is in ferment, and I think this is simply reflected in humor."

The silent generation of the 1950s was indeed giving way to the irreverent generation of the 1960s and the 1970s. Arthur Gelb of the *New York Times* called the new crop of comedians "modern evangelists. . . . The keynote of their satire is iconoclasm; they are out to shock people into an awareness of what is going on around them."

Contributing to the rapid spread of the new comedy was, of course, the all-persuasive influence of television. By 1969, most American homes watched television more than five hours a day, and the figure was going up. "The average child, before he enters first grade," said an F.C.C. commissioner, "spends more time in front of the TV set than he will getting his B.A. degree."

Pat Paulsen, who possessed "the deadest pan since Buster Keaton," ran for the presidency in 1968 on a peace platform. "Let them sell guns, but no bullets," was his answer to the gun control issue.

When cowboys took over television entertainment in the 1950s and early 1960s, comedians took flight. And when the rage for boots and spurs began to abate, the spy season opened. An epidemic of intrigue, violence, and sex became standard television fare.

However, as the years passed, a return to comedy, both sophisticated and unsophisticated, took place. More often than not, it was a different kind of laugh making: topical, angry, often shocking. Whether the medium was television, stage, screen, or records, comedians increasingly were reflecting a world around them knee deep in crises.

"Comedy is not an isolated thing," said Milt Kamen, stand-up comic. "It is something that has to do with our daily lives, the whole country's life, the world's life."

There began to appear a rebirth of topical humor. Mimics of famous political personalities found appreciative audiences. David Frye was one who demonstrated amazing ability to imitate and

146

exaggerate voices and facial expressions of those he would hold up to ridicule. "People long to laugh at their leaders," he was quoted as saying. "Audiences need a way to vent their feelings and fears about these big, political figures, and they can do it with me...."

Another comedian to win popularity by caricature was Don Adams in the television serial "Get Smart." As the bumbling secret agent, Adams evidently supplied viewers with welcome relief from the hordes of implausible spies that had descended upon them. Another foe of pomposity and fraud was Pat Paulsen, a sad-eyed comedian whose vague resemblance to a basset hound masked skillful comedy techniques.

Paulsen achieved national recognition on the "Smothers Brothers Comedy Hour," where his ironic "editorials" helped him steal part of the show from better-known comedians. Paulsen's sensitive timing permitted even doubtful jokes to seem hilarious. Claiming to have been a school-boy athlete, Paulsen would solemnly inform his TV audience that "in high school, I was a four-letter word."

The "Smothers Brothers Comedy Hour" itself marked something of a milestone in modern American comedy. While Tom and Dick Smothers had achieved a reputation for their particular brand of fun making, it was only in the period of the late 1960s that the brothers began veering sharply toward the area of political commentary. Perhaps it was because they were young and the youth of America lacked spokesmen on television networks. Perhaps it simply was the fact that the brothers felt strongly about

Politics and comedy mixed when David Frye did his imitations of Richard M. Nixon and Lyndon B. Johnson.

One of television's more offbeat popular comedy shows: Dan Rowan and Dick Martin's "Laugh-In," featuring Goldie Hawn, successor to Gracie Allen's comic laurel; Arte Johnson, sinister German soldier and dirty old man; Theresa Graves; and Henry Gibson. Not pictured are Alan Sues; Joanne Worley; Ruth Buzzi; and the solo artist, Lily Tomlin.

current issues. At any event, the Smothers Brothers' humor increasingly involved controversial issues and entertainers of the day.

In the spring of 1969, a CBS announcement was made that the "Smothers Brothers Comedy Hour" had been cancelled. A network spokesman stated: "The central issue involved here is whether a broadcast organization has some responsibility to the public with respect to questions of taste. . . ."

Stated Tom Smothers: "While our cities burn, young people watch documentaries on the efficacy of our government. . . ."

The Dick Gregory of the late 1960s and early 1970s was somewhat different from the earlier nightclub entertainer. In addition to having longer hair and a beard, Gregory was more militant and more insistent upon bringing forward issues which he felt vital. Gregory largely gave up the nightclub for engagements on college and university campuses.

If Dick Gregory became the most widely known black comedian since Bert Williams, he was merely the first of a growing number of nationally known black laughmakers who gained prominence

Goldie Hawn

Arte Johnson

Theresa Graves

Henry Gibson

Dick Gregory combined laugh making with a social conscience. "I began taking more and more time off from being a funnyman," he said, "to help my people."

in this era. In reality, many black comedians were new only to whites. "The line that leads to Moms Mabley, Nipsey Russell, Dick Gregory, Bill Cosby and myself," stated Godfrey Cambridge, "can be traced back to the satire of slave humor, back even through minstrelsy. . . ."

Cambridge pointed out how around the 1940 era, large numbers of black families came from the South to northern urban centers. Black entertainers became more frequent and black comedians "were speaking more and more the common, inside humor of the streets. . . . For the first time, a Negro comedian became a hero. . . . All of a sudden, there was no more shuffle. . . ."

Another of the more popular black comedians was Flip Wilson, whose casual laugh making hid a carefully structured technique. "Do you want to build a $50,000 home and some Indian build a wigwam next to it?" he would ask his audience. "I never heard of anybody playing cowboys and colored people."

For decades, some of the nation's most able comedians seldom were known beyond Harlem and other ghetto areas. Among these was Moms Mabley, black comedienne, who became a popular national entertainer on television and on records late in life.

Once asked how she goes about her laugh making, Moms replied: "I just tell folks the truth. If they don't want the truth, then don't come to Moms. Anybody that comes to me, I'll help 'em. I don't say anything I don't mean."

Still another prominent comedian of the 1970s was Bill Cosby, the first black entertainer to have a featured role in a regular television program. "My whole career took a big turn from the time Dick Gregory made it five or six years ago," Cosby stated. An athlete in school, Cosby found he had a natural inclination toward comedy, but more important than that, an intimate knowledge of

Too rarely have films achieved high levels of comedy in the 1960s and early 1970s. Among recent all-time box-office hits were: It's a Mad, Mad, Mad, Mad World *(at right);* The Graduate *(above); and* The Russians Are Coming, The Russians Are Coming *(below).*

Cleavon Little, Harvey Korman, and Mel Brooks in a scene from Blazing Saddles, *a wacky western.*

ordinary people, particularly the underprivileged. Cosby was able to provide a special, gentle type of humor, both satirical and understanding at the same time.

Racial slurs and stereotypes, once accepted by performers and audiences alike, became taboo. But cultural differences have been exaggerated with humor, laughingly providing new insight into variations in the human condition. Bill Cosby, Dick Gregory, Flip Wilson, Redd Foxx, Jimmie Walker, and other black artists presented to millions of people the unique comedy that emerged from black misery and the need to find relief in laughter.

The new comedy—black and white—gave birth to one of television's most successful shows in "Laugh-In," a weekly collection of rapid-fire satire and lunacy.

"Laugh-In" was a frenetic successor to "This Was The Week

Jonathan Winters was one of the most gifted of modern satirists. His versatility caused him to be called the "one man repertory company."

Bill Cosby became the first black entertainer with a regular starring role in a television series.

That Was," which engaged in effective political satire before its sudden curtailment a few years previous. "Laugh-In" provided television comedy with one of its more creative technological approaches since the days of Ernie Kovacs. A mixture of physical comedy and social comment, the revue rushed through its weekly hour so breathlessly that it was difficult to recall what happened when it was all over.

Joke followed joke at such a pace that, if the viewers missed one, they need not worry; another would be along any second. That is not to say that all or even most of the jokes had merit; it simply did not seem to matter.

"Laugh-In" made use, to an unprecedented extent, of cutting-room techniques to avoid boredom and to leave the viewer hungry for more. The show bore a resemblance to a sophisticated, many-

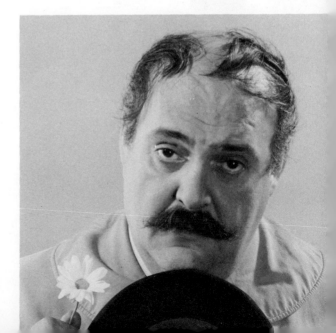

Zero Mostel, one of the more creative of modern comedians, believes that, "the freedom of any society varies with the size of its laughter."

ringed circus. Winner of six Emmy awards, Dan Rowan and Dick Martin, part owners of "Laugh-In," evidently believed there was safety in speed. For once, the commercials supplied a welcome moment of relative sanity.

The success of such television fare explained the growing plight of those nightclubs that flourished during the era when meaningful laugh making was a TV rarity.

Moreover, the rewards of television not only tempted comedians from nightclubs. "Comedy is now non-existent in practically all standard burlesque theaters," stated *Variety*, "for the very good reason that the shows no longer have any comedians, good or bad, only strippers, good or bad."

Television was also the culprit behind the holocaust that hit Hollywood years ago. People simply found it more convenient and cheaper to sit at home and laugh at television comedians than pay at a motion picture box office. Struggling for its existence, the movies responded by seeking a specialized field, difficult for the home television to match. They found it, more or less, in violence and sex.

While there have been successful film comedies in recent years, the list of *Variety*'s "All Time Box Office Champs" contains significantly few modern films that owed their success primarily to laughmakers. Television, inevitably, had similar influence on the legitimate theater, largely represented by Broadway and off-

Mary Tyler Moore

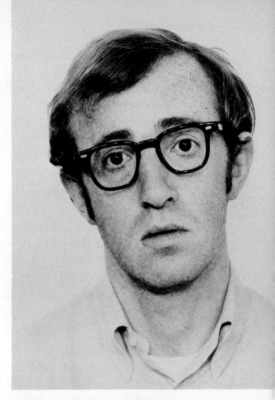

Woody Allen

Broadway productions. Interestingly, Mike Nichols and Elaine May, the one-time hilarious record-making comedy team, each independently had a finger in a number of productions in the theater and motion pictures. Another one of the rare successful

Flip Wilson

producers of comedy, Neil Simon, indicated the trend toward content on Broadway:

"Humor isn't anything if it can't make you think and feel," he stated in *Newsweek.* "Anyone can make a baby laugh by shaking a rattle in its face. I don't want to write for infants and shake rattles."

Thus, if the living theater had its share of comedy, it was largely based upon the talent of its writers rather than the personality of its comedians. Television not only captured most of the talented comedians of the period, but also subtly influenced the content of their humor. The stand-up comedian was at first more or less the prisoner of the microphone. He employed minimum help from costume, setting, or physical antics, but depended mostly on verbal jokes and his ability to tell them, a carry over from the master of ceremonies in the summer hotels or borscht circuit and the nightclubs.

Another phenomenon of television, applying particularly but by no means exclusively to the stand-up comedian, was the strategic role of the comedy writer behind the scenes.

Of course, the comedy writer has always been of considerable, if unappreciated, importance to the comedian. While certain laughmakers, such as Fred Allen, wrote much of their own material, an increasing number have depended upon gag writers. For years, Bob Hope was one of the nation's most celebrated comedians by virtue of his rapid-fire delivery, an accomplishment not only based upon his own special brazen talent as a stand-up comedian, but also the result of those who prepared his often side-splitting commentary. When asked once who was the most influential person in her life, Lucille Ball thought briefly and replied: "My writers."

Once when confronted in public by the sharp wit of Fred Allen, Jack Benny replied: "You wouldn't say that if my writers were here."

Further evidence that social issues have had a great impact on comedy has been the emergence of a series of talented and very different female comic artists. There have been the comic antics of Bea Arthur in "Maude," Esther Rolle in "Happy Days," and Carol Burnett, all carry overs from Martha Raye and Fanny Brice. But among the new women have been found some who tackled women's issues, poking fun at the old ways. Joan Rivers had a

Jack Lemmon

Richard Pryor

Don Adams

Alan King

Moms Mabley

Godfrey Cambridge

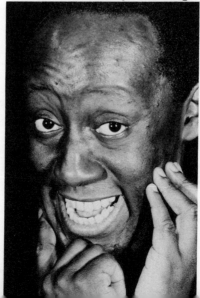

Anne Meara and Jerry Stiller   *Don Rickles*

running stream of one-line jokes or quick situations in which she made fun of herself. She was a loser by not playing woman's traditional role with success and because of her own faults. Anne Meara is a funny lady almost as real and much more clever than our neighbors in dealing with ordinary situations in everyday life.

Most unusual among the new women is Lily Tomlin, who has made the great leap from television variety shows to a one-person Broadway enchantment called "Appearing Nightly." She has fast become an unofficial spokesperson for the women's movement. Lily, as she is affectionately known to many, has created characters and personalities in her sketches to carry the message in many guises; telephone operator, society lady, small child, four persons in a single's bar, and others. According to reviewer Clive Barnes, she is "Fantasy gone sane. She is a woman's eye view of

Phyllis Diller

madness. Her feminism is essential—she is so flamboyantly female she can make fun of the fact. And she can be gamine and cute. . . . She defines herself and her times."

One of her characters reflects everyone's confused childhood from a child's view. In "Lies My Mother Taught Me," she brought a roar from the audience with the line, "Whatever makes you happy makes me happy." She makes fun of herself as an aspiring actress receiving direction from an expert waitress—her other self—in how to live straight and honest by waiting on table. She can make fun with religion, television commercials, and conscience, with quadraplegics or sex without hurting anyone. She is the feminists' comic when she says, "Every time I see a yield sign on the highway, I feel sexually threatened" or "There is nothing natural about natural childbirth."

As a one-woman entertainer, she is a female phenomenon. Her content includes all varieties of social satire from one-line jokes to body humor and quick role changes. Her audience is a youthful one and lively in its response. She gets laughs and standing ovations as well. When all scheduled performances were sold out, she allowed the run to be extended. Such a workout for an individual performer might suggest an endurance contest with herself.

Carroll O'Connor (Archie Bunker) became TV's most widely watched and most controversial comedian of his era. He is shown with Rob Reiner and Sally Struthers, who (together with Archie's wife played by Jean Stapleton) also starred in "All in the Family."

For Lily it seems, in her own style, a love affair with an ever-changing audience.

Tomlin has an advantage over performers who play for filming alone. Critic Kenneth Tynan said, "There is nothing so disastrous for the comedian as playing comedy with nothing coming back from the audience—for the performer, there has to be that bubble of laughter. On television, there are the cameramen, the lighting people, the directors. These are nonrespondents, technicians."

But the film medium has used material so fast that the old timers' acts were overexposed in a few short seasons. It then became the playground for more serious humor, presented with lightness and skill by blacks, Hispanics, and women.

If television has extended its influence into almost every area of comedy, there is one region where it has not exerted as much influence. This is the area of what some call "sick" laugh making. Whether television standards will be changed in the future, it cannot be said. Nevertheless, up to the beginning of the 1970s, television had considered itself primarily family entertainment as far as comedy was concerned. Hence, the sick jokes which invaded the theater, the records, and the nightclubs were largely off the air waves. Nevertheless, they comprised a significant influence on American comedy. "Sex is no longer a taboo topic," stated *Time* as early as 1966. "It is, in fact, one of the commonest. Humor has not only been firmly entrenched in the bedroom, but is increasingly being brought into the bathroom."

Speaking of the trend toward sick comedy, Alan King, the comedian, stated: "I wasn't so shocked at the comedian or what he was saying. I was shocked at the audience laughing at what he was saying. That's what frightened me. That there is a market for this. They talk about cave-ins and atomic fall-out. The fact that sick comics are succeeding today . . . that's what frightens me!"

One of the most successful and probably most talented of the so-called sick comedians was Lenny Bruce. According to Ralph J. Gleason, editor of *Jazz*, Bruce was actually a voice "dissenting from the world gone mad. . . . His colossal irreverence punctures the hypocrisy of religion, politics and other areas with an arrow tipped with poison."

When Bruce was hauled into court for using obscenity in public entertainment, the prosecution based its case on the argument

The TV series "M*A*S*H" used comedy applied to intense hurt and human drama. Outstanding in the fine cast are Alan Alda and Gary Burghoff.

that the purpose of comedy was to get laughs, and that Bruce's performance wasn't funny. Bruce simply had indulged in the use of obscenity for obscenity's sake. The defense, which won acquittal, produced witnesses who testified that Bruce's work on the stage had "redeeming social significance," and that an obscene word had to be considered in this context and not in isolation.

Commenting on trends in entertainment, Groucho Marx once stated: "I don't think you have to show love making on the screen any more than you have to show bowel movements. . . . When I heard about 'Hair,' I was kind of curious about the six naked primates on stage," Groucho stated in a *New York Times* interview, "so I called at the box office, and they said that tickets were $11 a piece. That's an awful price to pay. I went to my bathroom at home, took off my clothes and looked at the mirror for five minutes, and I said, 'This isn't worth $11.'"

One comic artist rarely seen on the medium he uses more often than any other producer is Norman Lear. Not a funnyman, nonetheless he has given a start in concept or controversial idea to a great variety of television situation comedies that have changed the nature of what is permissible and possible for home viewing. Lear has presented the comic side of pressing social problems such as racial prejudice, urban violence, sexual freedom, religious bigotry, war, poverty, changing life styles, and many more. What are these social issues doing in comedy time, a part of entertainment that supposedly was out of bounds for such serious ideas?

Norman Lear, in an interview that appeared in *Signature*, June, 1975, said, "The theory behind most material on television when I was learning the business was that the average viewer wanted

161

Redd Foxx as Fred Sanford in "Sanford and Son," the TV comedy success of the 1970s.

diversion from his problems, mindless escapist entertainments, illusions, not the realities of life. But my experience is that the leadership of this country—including politicians as well as network executives—consistently underestimates the American public. People love to see somebody else with their problems."

The reason we can laugh at the conflicts, the arguments, the dilemmas of Archie, Maude, the Jeffersons, Mary Hartmann, The Fonz, kids and teacher in Mr. Kotter's classes is that they are so much like ourselves in what they face. And so clever in their solutions.

Credit must go to Norman Lear and the entire production

Beatrice Arthur starred as "Maude" in the TV comedy series. She is shown here with Bill Macy who plays her husband, Walter.

The antics of Jimmie Walker, a character in a family situation comedy, "Good Times," set a distinctive comic style which is imitated by thousands, black and white.

companies, not just to the comedians alone, for bringing sensitive subjects into the realm of comedy for audiences in the millions.

When Redd Foxx transplanted his lovable character into San- ford and Son, he and his backers helped to open up a whole new area previously considered taboo, ethnic humor. The big change in ethnic humor is the warmth, the personal and universal quali- ties that are expressed in a variety of special ethnic ways. The flavor or the taste of a folk style comes right into the homes of people who are stuck with their prejudices from the past. Ten years ago it would have seemed like a joke—and one not in good taste—for a president of the United States to be seen talking to

"Professor" Irwin Corey was famous for making simple stories complicated beyond belief.

Sherman Hemsley, Isabel Sanford, and Diane Sommerfield of "The Jeffersons."

the people of the country wearing a casual sweater, an informal shirt and slacks, and a big, friendly grin. Improbable? It happened, and on television.

Henry Winkler, popular as the television character "The Fonz," is a professionally trained actor now turning to serious drama.

15

What's Funny Now?

Just as the earliest comedians found their funny ideas in everyday life, so do today's comic heroes. The situations are different in an age of technology, but relationships between people are the same. But are they?

Looking backward, when the country farmer type of comic personality exemplified by the Jonathan figure broke through the Puritan moral attitude, he also established an American style of humor.

Between then and now there have been a variety of comic styles and personalities that have made Americans laugh, but some that were once popular seem to have disappeared.

Remnants of earlier styles, however, may be seen in different settings or disguises. The ethnic humor which made fun of an immigrant's accent or mannerisms of speech or of the ignorance of the newcomers to America became rare.

Whatever became of the prissy miss or the slapstick, or the comic chase, or making a person look small or hurt in order to make a situation funny?

The minstrel show as professional entertainment has disappeared. Black humor in public has changed more radically than any other form. What happened to the loose-limbed, eccentric dancer in blackface, the stereotyped dialogue of the minstrel men? These forms have been replaced in black comedy in several ways. Making fun of one's own weaknesses and fears as blacks once did privately was put forward by such performers as Flip Wilson and Redd Foxx in self-deprecating stories and jokes.

In addition, the unique style and elegance of American music that derived from black music has had an impact on all American theater including comedy.

The most persistent feature that has carried through American humor across the two centuries can be seen in the evolution of the country comic, the Jonathan. He was not only unlike the clumsy dolt of old-world crude comedy or pantomime, but he established an American tradition that has evolved over time into newer forms. He was a neighborly looking type who fooled with and fooled his audiences, being so much like them.

Not too different were such ethnic jokesters as Weber and Fields, who made fun of themselves, their own people, and their ethnic background. They sometimes joked about themselves, but very often told stories that were demeaning to others. Racial slurs were coarsely comic and widely accepted in anecdotes based more on stereotypes than fact.

As early burlesque lost its refinement and became slapstick, other comics had already learned from burlesque the use of body movement for caricature to communicate an illusion of reality. Red Skelton for many years combined the Jonathan figure with pantomime, which has become increasingly accepted as a comic form.

The stand-up comedians with the line of fast chatter are today's minstrel men with no need to paint their faces. They wear tuxedos or ordinary clothes. Dress-up comics no longer needed, in recent years, to wear comic hats like Ed Wynn or fancy clothes like Milton Berle. Costumes have been worn when a comic wishes to assume special characteristics like Carol Burnett's scrub woman, or the female impersonations of Flip Wilson.

Pantomime has become, too, a part of the scene in the most casual of theaters. Young people, training themselves in their art, with no theaters in which to perform, are using the streets. In big and noisy cities, clusters of people have gathered on street corners to watch jugglers, dancers, clowns, and many kinds of mimicry. The response has been direct—applause, some money, and then viewers continue on their way. This ancient and universal open air entertainment seems to have taken hold in parts of the United States. The content, if not the comic techniques, is part of the present time. The comics attack with humor serious subjects: war, murder, government, corruption in high places, as well as common human weaknesses and frustrated desires.

When Mort Sahl reintroduced jibes and jokes about political issues and figures, he stimulated a new wave of social satire. Social satire was given public recognition at the Democratic National Convention in 1976 in a film shown before the delegates and to television viewers at home. Ed Asner, a well-known television actor of comic roles, played what was probably his comic master-piece when he did scenes from "Mr. Dooley in Peace and War," a monologue taken from humorous stories of the last century by Peter Finley Dunne.

Even the bitter comedy of the late Lenny Bruce was funny, if peculiarly his own. The critic Kenneth Tynan said of him, "He is seldom funny without an ulterior motive. He makes you squirm as you smile. He breaks through the barriers of laughter to the horizons beyond where truth has its sanctuary."

Bruce tried to shock people into serious awareness of racism, hunger, murder by war, deprivation, and violations of human dignity.

With the rise of consciousness, there has been a refinement of understanding of human relationships. If that seems absurd, all one must do is look at what is funny now on the American TV screen.

There is a new format for the one-line comic and that seems to be as a master of ceremonies or a guest in a TV variety show. Personalities present acts not very different from some of the old stage vaudeville acts of the earlier part of the twentieth century. Some say that old-time vaudeville still lives—in Las Vegas. But most people today share a common experience in humor or comedy style and they find it without leaving home. One family situation comedy features a man with a distinctly Irish name living with his Polish named son-in-law, each laughing at the other, but at human foibles and not at racial slurs. Black families, the working class, the well-to-do, and professionals such as psy-chiatrists and teachers, all come in for their share of the fun.

Some of the special characteristics of people from different parts of the country or from other countries have been incorporated in the family and other situation comedies that have proliferated on television. Chicanos and Puerto Ricans, Italians, Irish, Poles, Easterners, country folk from the country and the farms, all have become a part of everyday life in America through exposure on television, bound to the viewer through shared laughter. The comics take what is unique to a given culture, like Esther Rolle in her many roles as a mature black woman, and present a farcical interpretation of the way life really is. In life, these events may not be very funny, but looking and laughing makes life bearable. Situation comedies have become also a parody of life as we would like it to be. Get-rich-quick schemes that don't work are an old-time comic act renewed with a little ethnic zest, for example. Reaching millions of people in a way that gets quickly to the heart of the matter, through sharing common hopes and weaknesses, has served to cut across the many and intense social, economic, and racial barriers of the past.

Bringing personal, racial, and ethnic issues out into the open with kindness instead of mockery set a pattern that permitted political satire and social criticism to reach enormous numbers of people, again in the most personal and bearable way, through humor. Not only do stand-up comedians in nightclubs or as guests in interview programs deal penetratingly with serious subjects, but these topics have also appeared with clear intent to question accepted notions and to provoke response from a wide audience in situation comedies. Questions about racial bias, marriage and the family, numbers of children affordable in a family, promiscuity, mental illness, mutual trust, honorable behavior, and even how to have a good family fight have been presented in recent years. This goes far beyond the wit of Will Rogers, for example, but remains in that tradition of social commentary.

Perhaps a reason why Charlie Chaplin remained popular with younger generations was that his comedy gave expression to what was on many a youthful mind: "More than machinery, we need humanity," he said. "More than cleverness, we need kindness and gentleness. . . . We want to live by each other's happiness—not by each other's misery. We don't want to hate and despise one another. In this world, there is room for everyone. And the good earth is rich and can provide for everyone."

Sometimes it takes the special genius of a comic actor among the characters to bring alive what might be an ordinary parody of life among our neighbors. It is that timing, that imitation and slight exaggeration of the way people present themselves to each other, that ear for the sound of what is funny and the quick tongue to make sure we all hear it that way, that is the comic art.

In order to study the impact of the most recent and penetrating modes of comedy, a survey was made of students aged fifteen to seventeen years old. One group of 650 lived just one hundred miles from New York City, the home of nightclubs, television studios, gag writers, and funny waiters in restaurants. Not one percent of these students had been outside of their home state. But as young adults, they have much in common with the rest of America. In describing their favorite funny people, most references were to comics who had television exposure. The range was from old movie clown types all the way to the most recent madness of a British import, "Monty Python's Flying Circus." While the students enjoyed one-line jokes from members of their families, they spent most of their TV time viewing situation comedies featuring highly developed comic artists. There seemed to be no racial bias in choosing black artists along with white. They all represented something close to home in situations that were not unimaginable. The funny situations did not take place in gaudy nightclubs, but in familiar settings in which the youths could imagine themselves. The comic style, the timing, the self-deprecating joke, the sharing of a special insight has become more universal based on these common experiences via television.

When asked what was funny in their everyday lives, some students acknowledged that it was the name of their school, Coginchaug. Unusual place names always were guaranteed to get a laugh in many parts of America and still do.

Many students have learned to view their own experiences as funny only after parroting the comics on film or television. Almost no one has ever seen a comedian in the flesh. Yet every student in an English class has seen Bill Cosby narrating a film called *Black History, Lost, Strayed or Stolen*, in which he traces American

"Good night, folks, and good night, Mrs. Calabash, wherever you are."

comic style and the tragedies of stereotyping along with other history. Always straight and sometimes bitterly true, the impact of the film is mostly on white students, since only four in the town are black. The students did not discriminate between black or white performers, but emphasized rather that some used body language, did funny things with their faces, stood up and talked, and so on.

All agreed, however, that Mr. Kotter, the unpretentious teacher in a television school situation comedy, would be an ideal teacher and that a class full of comic types was not unfunny. Few, even the most talented, saw themselves as capable of carrying out those roles, but were able to enjoy the comic artist's version of their reality. They liked to see ordinary people in absurd situations, to see people in positions of large or petty authority break down before them, to be anti-establishment without penalty, to say words that you are not supposed to say, to get hysterical over ordinarily acceptable contradictions such as jumbo/shrimp or military/intelligence, or to throw around one's body as if it were made of rubber and have it bounce back.

For these students, the unreal inner-city high school becomes a part of their own lives through the magic of the comic's art and the humor of an almost familiar situation. This is not far removed from the earliest American comic—the Jonathan character which some farmers, two hundred years ago, didn't think could possibly be funny, so true to life he was at that time.

Regardless of taste in comedy—always a sensitive area—one fact is indisputable: there have been changes. According to Abel Green, veteran *Variety* editor, "No question that today's comedy is less physical and more cerebral. No question that the Will Rogers' brand of 'topics' from the headlines, presumably gauged at the lofty *Ziegfeld Review* trade, has long since been multiplied by dozens of equally effective comedians . . . for much wider appreciation."

It has been said that the most important function of humor is to render a person more compassionate and understanding of fellow people. Indeed, it is difficult to be hostile and humorous at the same time.

Mark Twain put the matter this way:

"The human race, in its poverty, has unquestionably one really effective weapon—laughter. . . . Against the assault of laughter, nothing can stand."

Afterword

William Cahn died before he had a chance to complete this book. He was a valiant and a funny man who believed that humor and women were made expressly to bring delight and flavor to life in its most relevant forms. He wanted everyone he knew to appreciate the wit and humor he was aware of in each of them: acquaintance, friend, reader, public figure.

Because he had dedicated the original book from which this was taken to me—after all, I was his best audience—and because I had done much of the early research along with him; and especially because I knew one of his secret dreams for himself—that was to be able to swing a lariat like Will Rogers and tell a slow, funny, political joke at the same time—for these reasons, I wanted to complete in some concrete way what he had enjoyed so profoundly.

Acknowledgments

Writing about comedy is a serious affair. The most liberal reader and broad-minded critic can become relentless when their standards of humor are violated. And violate them we have. Space alone made this necessary. Since there were judgments to be made, we made them. For such judgments, kindly blame us; not the following, whose counsel, assistance, and encouragement we appreciate.

Among the people who helped were Mrs. Annie Stein, Abel Green, Harold Lloyd, Ed Wynn, Steve Allen, Mack Sennett, Sam Levenson, Harry Birdoff, Norman Franklin, Richard Maney, Sol Jacobson, Sally Powers, and many others.

Hundreds of books and countless periodicals and newspapers were, naturally, consulted in putting together this work. Among those books which, in retrospect, appear to have been most useful are included: *Show Biz* by Abel Green and Joe Laurie, Jr., Henry Holt & Company, New York, 1942; *The Merry Partners, the Age and Stage of Harrigan and Hart,* by E. J. Kahn, Jr., Random House, New York, 1955. *Weber and Fields,* by Felix Isman, Boni & Liveright, New York, 1924; *King of Comedy,* by Mack Sennett, Doubleday & Company, Garden City, 1954; *My Life Is in Your Hands,* by Eddie Cantor, Harper & Bros., New York, 1928; *Schnozzola,* by Gene Fowler, The Viking Press, New York, 1951; *George M. Cohan,* by Ward Moorehouse, J. B. Lippincott Company, Philadelphia, 1943; *Charlie Chaplin,* by Theodore Huff, Abelard-Schuman, Ltd., New York, 1951; *Will Rogers,* by P. J. O'Brien, John C. Winston Company, Philadelphia, 1935; *W. C. Fields,* by Robert Lewis Taylor, Doubleday & Company, Garden City, 1949; *The Marx Brothers,* by

177

Acknowledgments

Kyle Crichton, Doubleday & Company, Garden City, 1950; *Life with Groucho*, by Arthur Marx, Popular Library, New York, 1955; *Nigger*, by Dick Gregory, Pocket Books, New York, 1965; *The Great Comedians Talk about Comedy*, Larry Wilde, The Citadel Press, 1968; *Sixty Years of American Humor*, edited by Joseph Lewis French, Little Brown & Company, Boston, 1924; *The Treasurer's Report*, by Robert Benchley, Harper & Bros., New York, 1930.

The extract on Page 75 is from *Charlie Chaplin* by Theodore Huff, Abelard-Schuman.

The extract on Page 100 is from *The Treasurer's Report* by Robert Benchley, Harper & Brothers. Copyright 1930 by Robert Benchley.

Additional advice and encouragement came from Iris Rosoff, who made this edition possible. In preparing this material after the death of Bill Cahn, Rhoda Cahn wishes to thank Eileen Reilly, Betty Van Witsen and Phyllis Johnson, Elaine Reilly and Robert Reilly for personally sharing the old jokes and providing moral support.

Picture acknowledgements are due many sources including the following:

Museum of the City of New York, 15 (left), 18, 39, 47, 61
Library of Congress, 22, 57 (top)
Paramount, frontispiece, 65 (bottom), 69, 75, 81, 100, 104 (top), 107
  (bottom), 109 (top), 117 (top), 119, 144, 164 (bottom)
H. Blair, 35
NBC, 53, 91, 113, 114, 115, 117 (bottom), 120 (top), 123, 125, 132 (top),
  142 (top left, bottom left), 143 (top left), 146, 148, 149, 153 (top),
  155 (bottom), 158 (bottom), 162 (top)
RKO General Pictures, 55, 98, 103 (top)
Universal, 58 (bottom), 59, 84 (bottom), 103 (bottom), 143 (top right)
Warner Bros., 60, 87, 89, 104 (bottom), 152 (top)
Museum of Modern Art, 63, 64, 65 (top), 68, 70, 73, 80, 92, 95, 97
20th Century-Fox, 67, 84 (top)
Clarence Sinclair Bull, 82
Hal Roach, 83, 85 (top)
MGM, 99, 107 (top), 141 (middle right)
Columbia Pictures, 101, 141 (top left), 157 (top left), 169
Vitagraph, 102 (bottom), 141 (top right)
Mercury Artists Corp., 110, 157 (bottom left)
Barney Stein, 111
CBS, 120 (bottom), 126, 127, 128, 129, 132 (bottom), 133, 135, 141 (bot-
  tom right), 142 (top right), 143 (bottom left, bottom right), 147, 154,
  157 (bottom right), 159, 161, 162 (bottom), 163 (top), 164 (top)
MGM Verve Records, 131 (bottom)
Waukegan News-Sun, 138
United Artists, 77, 141 (middle left), 151 (top, bottom)
Sheldon Secunda, 150
Embassy Pictures, 151 (middle)
Max Waldman, 153 (bottom)
Berk Costello, 157 (top right)
Dan Miller, 163 (bottom)
Capitol Records Inc., 141 (bottom left)
Theatre Collection, The New York Public Library at Lincoln Center, Astor,
  Lenox and Tilden Foundations, 54, 109 (bottom)
Photo provided by Franklin D. Roosevelt Library, 72
Reprinted with permission from the Minneapolis Tribune, 74, 83 (top)
© 1973 Walt Disney Productions, 85 (bottom)
Bob Young, Jr., Georgetown University, 139
Harold Lloyd stills provided courtesy of Time-Life Films, Inc., 79, 80
© 1978 American Broadcasting Companies, Inc., 135

Index

Numbers in boldface type refer to photographs

About the Authors

Bill Cahn, growing up in New York City, had an opportunity to see many of the major vaudeville performers take their turns at major theaters and movie houses. When his family sent him down along Broadway on a Saturday afternoon to report the names of "stars" at the local theater, he would often return saying that he had read on the marquee, "Cooler Inside Than Out."

That joke was enough to gain him the price of admission. Many years later, when, as a professional writer, he wrote biographies of Harold Lloyd and Jimmy Durante (*Harold Lloyd's World of Comedy* and *Goodnight Mrs. Calabash, Wherever You Are*), he was able to relive those hours of wonder and merriment.

Throughout his life Bill Cahn practiced magic tricks, learned to swing a lariat and tell droll tales in the style of Will Rogers, and mixed social commentary with humor. This was one step removed from the humor of his Mississippi parents and uncles. They told gross and sometimes crude country tales originating deep in the heart of the American Southland. But they laughed together at themselves.

Rhoda Cahn did original research in American comedy with Bill. This research was academic in the sense of finding information but personal in the enjoyment of Bill's mimicry of those comics he had seen on stage in his youth. Rhoda Cahn's family was given to occasional imitations of the greats, Jolson and Jessel, but her family preferred sitting around the dining room table telling stories of immigrants and their funny ways of adapting in the "New World." Saturday movies were considered an avoidable evil, and vaudeville was a treat at the Poli Palace Theater stop on the vaudeville circuit. In New Haven, where Mrs. Cahn was born and raised, the "legit" theater had more status than the "slip-slop" comedian, especially in an immigrant family where learning the "best" of America was so important.

Rhoda and Bill Cahn collaborated and produced three children, numerous pieces of journalism, and three books for children. Together they did *The Story of Writing From Cave Art to Computer* and *No Time for School, No Time for Play: The Story of Child Labor in America.*

Bill Cahn was a professional journalist. He wrote about comedians and other American working people. When Rhoda Cahn is not writing for children, her own included, she is a psychologist in Connecticut, where the Cahn family has lived for many years.